REPARATIONS HANDBOOK

A practical approach to reparations for Black Americans

Intended to be used as a resource for understanding, advocating, and taking action

Chrissi Jackson

Thank You

Carl - for keeping me balanced

Mom & Dad - for your ongoing encouragement

©2021 Chrissi Jackson
All Rights Reserved
Manufactured in The United States of America

Cover Photograph by Chiamaka Nwolisa

Names: Chrissi Jackson, author
Includes bibliography of references.

Library of Congress Control Number: 2021913172

ISBN: 978-1-7372197-1-2 (Paperback)
ISBN: 978-1-7372197-2-9 (Hardcover)
ISBN: 978-1-7372197-0-5 (E-Book)

Dedication

To everyone who understands that race is only skin deep…

Everyone who acknowledges the value of cultural diversity…

For imaginations that reach beyond the scope of divided possibilities…

Those eager to step into the future, and explore the opportunities unveiled when humanity works together…

To everyone committed to shining a light on shadows
and willing to participate in proactive evolution…

We must understand how things came to be, understand what is broken, and consider our past when creating a better future.

Dear Readers,

Thank you for your time and interest in reparative justice.

i set out writing with the intention to create an educational tool that can be referenced when making a case for reparations for Black people in the United States. There is no way i could have anticipated how deflating - yet empowering - it would be to uncover African American history in the context of human rights. Hopefully, reading this history will also have an empowering impact on you.

A culture of White superiority is present in practically every facet of American life. Even while writing this book, i found myself overcoming the urge to tailor my message and methods to be palatable for White people. Recognizing how colonization continues to direct my thoughts and self-expression, i struggled to decide which parts of our traumatic history were necessary to include - if at all. Some historical harms must be revisited to prove the impact they have had across many generations. Some terrors, however, are so traumatic that reviewing them only perverts the pain and perpetuates their lingering effect. Ultimately, i decided to only include information necessary for understanding the African American experiences relevant to building a case for reparations. The case for reparations reaches far in every direction and the information included in this book merely scratches the surface. Nevertheless, i am confident it is enough for you to further research the topics that pique your interest.

Chapter one begins by defining reparations and outlining the United States' moral commitment to protect human rights and provide reparations for human rights violations.

Chapter two is a summary of slavery's impact on building the nation's foundation of wealth. Chapter three uncovers the culminating events that resulted in legalized segregation and unpacks its effect on Black families.

Chapter four, recaps the second largest migration in world history - The Great Migration. During this era, African American's left the South by the millions, integrated into the whole of the country, and redefined American culture.

In chapter five, we review acts of genocide against African Americans - many of which were racist attempts to eliminate Black people from the workplace and society. Chapter six reveals how the current criminal justice system is a natural evolution of convict leasing - a business that proved profitable by targeting Black citizens, incarcerating them, and leasing them to businesses. And chapter seven explores the causes and effects of the persistent racial wealth gap in the United States.

While reading chapters one through seven, i'd like to encourage you to think deeply about how the challenges African Americans have experienced throughout history parallel their modern-day challenges and experiences.

Finally, in chapter eight, we use the United Nations Basic Principles and Guidelines on the Right to a Remedy and Reparation as a guide for how both the US government and morally responsible community members can take action toward healing and repair.

For some, it can be difficult to discuss human rights violations committed against Black Americans by the United States without acknowledging the human rights violations committed against many other groups by the US. Personally, i am pro-equality, pro-reparations, and pro-replacing all systems that rely on oppression for success.

With that said, i urge you to stay focused on the topic at hand - reparations for Black Americans. Too often, the topic of reparations has been stalled, side-lined, and dismissed because expanding the conversation creates a problem so challenging it's dropped all together. We can successfully dismantle racism and repair the damage and division it's causing only if we advocate with clear goals.

It is essential to remember that our current racial hierarchy was intentionally created to divide the US. Together, we must revisit the past to understand the damage and learn how to repair it from the inside out. We must collectively, and individually, begin imagining the country we want to be now, and in the future - then begin creating and instilling new value systems. This can be a painful and challenging topic. Still, i encourage you to remain open-minded.

Table of Contents

One	Introducing… Reparations.	1
Two	America's Foundation of Wealth	8
Three	The Jim Crow Era	12
Four	Exodus: The Great Migration	28
Five	Genocide	34
Six	Slavery Evolved: the US Criminal Justice System	46
Seven	Stunted Growth: Exploring the Racial Wealth Gap	56
Eight	A Path Forward	66
	Sources and Recommended Reading	100

One

Introducing... Reparations.

We the people of the United States, in order to form a more perfect union, establish justice, insure domestic tranquility, provide for the common defense, promote the general welfare, and secure the blessings of liberty to ourselves and our posterity... have some work to do. The United States has always had a conflicting relationship with morality and White supremacy. But perhaps... do the same liberal, Christian, and capitalist values which create America's moral standards also instill the shame that causes us to dilute the impact of slavery on the country? The US is undeniably one of the most influential countries in the world - in part because of contributions in every field made by Black people. In more ways than one, African Americans serve as the backbone of the United States - all while persevering under fixed oppression. It is clear that the justice, tranquility, defense, welfare, and liberty described in our Constitution still guide the nation's moral compass, but at the ongoing expense of Black citizens.

In the colonial era, the United States enslaved Black people to build its infrastructure and continued to use them to build a foundation of wealth. After emancipation, the US legalized segregation and institutionalized privileges for people with white skin. The US authorized, left unpunished, and even participated in the mass murder of African Americans. US law enforcement continues to target Black communities to fill prisons for a profit. And a clear path to wealth-building remains obstructed for Black Americans.

Perpetuating this racial hierarchy - in our economy and society - not only keeps Black Americans from reaching their full potential, it inherently keeps everyone in the US from reaching their greatest potential. Cultural diversity is America's most valuable asset. Inevitably, the American Dream of a "perfect union" will not remain exclusive to White people. If we want to live up to the idea of being one of "the greatest nations in the world," we have to acknowledge institutionalized racism and work to eliminate it. We will only have the capacity to achieve our greatest potential once we uproot racism, level the economic playing field, and allow all citizens the equal opportunity to contribute to society.

The immoral truths about how this country came to be are shameful and painful to reckon with. But we must move forward with confidence in where we are, respect for those who were forced to sacrifice, and a clear vision and path for the country we aspire to be. The damage is done and we all know who the perpetrators and victims are. To focus on who to blame or who to pity is unproductive. Awarding reparations to African Americans for human rights violations is not an act of punishment or welfare. Awarding reparations is an act of remedy and repair. Awarding reparations is about understanding the causes and effects of the problem, taking accountability, and taking the necessary action to fix the damage and close the gaps - so that we can evolve beyond it.

Defining Reparations

N'COBRA defines reparations as a process of repairing, healing, and restoring people injured because of their group identity and in violation of their fundamental human rights by governments, corporations, institutions, and families.

The National Coalition of Blacks for Reparations in America, better known as N'COBRA, is a group of organizations and individuals organizing for the sole purpose of obtaining reparations for African descendants in the United States. This coalition has been at the forefront of educating the United States on reparations and developing pro-reparations legislation for the US Congress, including the bill H.R.40.

Please note: I specifically chose to lead with the N'COBRA definition of reparations because we must allow communities in need of repair to define reparations for themselves. In this case, we are talking about Black folk. Black people. African Americans. Black Americans. It is neither appropriate nor effective for the group that perpetrated or benefited from the violation to decide how the victims were affected and what an effective remedy will be. Yes, it will require the participation of all Americans to remedy and repair slavery's legacy of racism. Still, I would like to encourage all individuals who do not identify as Black to intentionally make space for Black people to lead conversations about reparations.

Introducing… Reparations.

Roots
Repair Nations. Reparations.

The word "reparations" itself is rooted in the word repair. The act of providing reparations has occurred for centuries. The first and continued form of reparations is given after a war - the losing side is obligated to pay the winner for lost land and other damages.

For example, after the Haitian Revolution - the 13-year war in which Haitian slaves fought against French colonists and won their independence - Haiti was ordered to pay 21 billion dollars in reparations to its former slave owners for the loss of their property and slaves. The irony of that example was intended. Here is another example: Eight months before President Lincoln signed the Emancipation Proclamation to end slavery in the United States, he signed The District of Columbia Emancipation Act - ordering the immediate emancipation of slaves in DC. This act compensated former slave owners up to $300 for each slave they freed, and distributed payments up to $100 for each freed slave who chose to leave the United States. In nine months, 930 petitions from former slave owners were approved for the freedom of 2,989 former slaves. To clarify, as a form of reparations, up to $896,700 were given to former slave owners in Washington DC, and zero dollars were given to former slaves who remained in the United States.

It was not until the mid-twentieth century that countries began providing reparations as a way of taking moral responsibility for violating human rights. For example, President Ronald Reagan signed a bill providing 20 thousand dollars per person, and an apology, to each living Japanese-American who was forced into concentration camps in the US during World War II.

Ultimately, it is up to the US Congress to decide which groups will be given reparations. Although Congress' selection process has proven to be biased, there are international guidelines that help identify when human rights have been violated and how to remedy and repair the harm caused.

The United States' Commitment to Protect Human Rights
In 1946, the United Nations General Assembly, including the United States of America, co-authored and adopted the Universal Declaration of Human Rights, also known as the UDHR. This document serves as a framework for defining fundamental human rights so that they can be protected. Since its creation, the UDHR continues to provide a basis for International Human Rights Law and obligates its adopters to honor its principles. A violation of these laws is not punishable by an international court. However, they are meant to serve as a nation's guidelines for moral accountability.

Article 4 of the UDHR reads, "No one shall be held in slavery or servitude; slavery and the slave trade shall be prohibited in all their forms."

Article 5 reads, "No one shall be subjected to torture or cruel, inhuman or degrading treatment or punishment."

And Article 8, "Everyone has the right to an effective remedy... for acts violating the fundamental rights granted him by the Constitution or by law."

By adopting the UDHR, the United States made a moral commitment to uphold and protect the human rights of all people - with the intention of promoting social progress, better standards of living, and an overall better world for everyone.

The United States' Commitment to Provide Remedy and Reparation

In 2005, the United Nations General Assembly, including the United States, co-authored and adopted the United Nations Basic Principles and Guidelines on the Right to a Remedy and Reparation for Victims of Gross Violations of International Human Rights Law and Serious Violations of International Humanitarian Law. These principles and guidelines affirm that victims of human rights violations should benefit from remedies and reparations in the form of restitution, compensation, rehabilitation, satisfaction, and a guarantee that it will not happen again.

Restitution should restore the victim to their original situation before the gross violations occurred and, as appropriate, include: restoration of liberty; enjoyment of human rights; restoring their identity, family life, and citizenship; returning them to their place of residence; restoration of employment; and return of property.

Compensation should be provided for any economic damage the violation caused, such as physical or mental harm; lost opportunities for employment, education, or social benefits; moral damage; and compensation for any costs required for legal or expert assistance, medicine, medical services, psychological services, and social services.

Rehabilitation should include medical and psychological care, as well as legal and social services.

Satisfaction should include, when appropriate, any or all of the following: taking effective measures towards stopping any continuing violations; verification of the facts and full public disclosure of the truth; assistance in the search for, recovery, identification, and reburial of the victim's bodies in accordance with their cultural practices; an official declaration or a judicial decision restoring their dignity,

Introducing... Reparations.

reputation and rights; a public apology including acknowledgment of the facts and acceptance of responsibility; a penalty against those responsible for the violations; tributes to the victims; and international humanitarian law training in educational material at all levels.

Guarantees of Non-Repetition should include, when appropriate, any or all of the following: strengthening the independence of the victims' justice system; protecting victims in legal, health-care, media, and human rights professions; providing society continual education of human rights and international humanitarian law; promoting and enforcing codes of conduct and ethical norms for public servants, law enforcement, correctional officers, economic enterprises, as well as media, medical, psychological, social service and military personnel; promoting mechanisms for preventing social conflicts and means for their resolutions; and reforming laws contributing to or allowing the human rights violations to happen.

When adopting these principles, the United States pledged a moral obligation to respect and implement International Human Rights Law (as defined in the UDHR) and to hold itself accountable when violating those laws by providing remedy and repair to the victims.

With commitments like these, it is curious why the United States refuses to provide reparations to its African American victims of gross human rights violations. The very gross human rights violations that built the foundation on which this country thrives.

The United States Has Never Been Opposed To Giving Reparations

When considering reparations for African Americans, it is important to acknowledge that the United States has never been opposed to giving reparations. There have been many times in our past where the sitting US government found it appropriate to grant reparations to its victims.

The following is a list of examples where reparations were provided to victims that suffered gross human rights violations committed by, and paid for by, the United States:

1971: The United States government granted 1 billion dollars and 44 million acres of land to Native Americans in the Alaska Natives Land Settlement.

1980: The United States government granted 81 million dollars to Native Americans in the Klamaths of Oregon Settlement.

1985: The United States government granted 105 million dollars to Native Americans in the Sioux of South Dakota Settlement.

1985: The United States government granted 12.3 million dollars to Native Americans in the Seminoles of Florida Settlement.

1985: The United States government granted 31 million dollars to Native Americans in the Chippewas of Wisconsin Settlement.

1988: President Ronald Reagan signed the Civil Liberties Act, granting a total of 1.2 billion dollars, and an apology, to approximately 80 thousand living Japanese-Americans who had been forced into concentration camps during World War II.

Additionally, 450 Aleuts were granted 12 thousand dollars per person, an apology, and 6.4 million dollars in a community trust for being placed in concentration camps during World War II.

1994: The state of Florida approved 2.1 million dollars for the living survivors of the Rosewood Massacre in 1923.

2012: The state of North Carolina committed to granting 50 thousand dollars to its living survivors of forced sterilizations, which took place between the 1920s and the 1970s.

2015: The city of Chicago signed into law an ordinance granting cash payments, free college education, and a range of social services - totaling 5.5 million dollars - to 57 living survivors of police torture. The ordinance also included a formal apology from Mayor Rahm Emanuel and a mandate to educate the broader public about the harm caused with a memorial and though public school curriculum.

2015: The state of Virginia committed to granting 25 thousand dollars to its living survivors of forced sterilizations that took place between the 1920s and the 1970s.

2018: The Supreme Court ordered that the state of Washington make billions of dollars worth of repairs to the roads where the state built culverts in a way that prevented salmon from swimming through and reaching their spawning grounds - which damaged the state's salmon habitats, contributed to population loss, and infringed upon a series of agreements, made in 1854 to 1855, in which Native American tribes in Washington State gave up millions of acres of land in exchange for "the right to take fish."

Introducing... Reparations.

As you see, the United States does not hold a policy against giving reparations - even for injustices that happened long ago. And The United Nations Basic Principles and Guidelines for Remedy and Reparation have clearly been referenced when granting reparations in the past. Yet, there has not been any effective forms of reparation formally given to African Americans for slavery or its legacy of continued racism and discrimination.

Taking Action

In 1989, Representative John Conyers introduced the bill H.R.40 to the United States Congress. H.R.40 is a bill that would establish a commission to study and develop reparation proposals for African Americans. The commission would examine slavery and discrimination, identify the role that federal and state governments had in supporting slavery and discrimination, investigate the lingering effects of slavery on living African Americans and society, then recommend appropriate remedies. To be clear, if passed, this bill would simply begin a study - an examination - of the effects of slavery. It would develop a proposal - simply ideas - for reparations. This bill has been proposed by members of every US Congress since 1989, but still has not passed.

Whether or not to provide reparations to African American's is not a question of America's willingness to provide reparations, it is a question of America's willingness to admit that slavery is wrong and against our moral ethics. Are we willing to recognize the damage that institutionalized racism is causing our society? Are we willing to repair the damage and rebuild a more equitable society? Are we willing to honor our commitment to protecting human rights?

Two

America's Foundation of Wealth

Slavery was the key that unlocked the United States' first fountain of wealth and allowed the country to quickly grow and thrive. Throughout history, many of the world's greatest civilizations were built by slaves. But the race-based chattel slavery system used in the Americas was particularly horrific. These slaves would be slaves for life, treated as personal possessions, and held no basic human rights. They were sold, traded, and managed as commodities by individuals, businesses, and institutions. The ability to buy and sell slaves, often on credit, was an opportunity for both individuals and institutions to fund the large-scale growth of their business - and jumpstarted generations of wealth-building. Furthermore, the rapid production of cotton produced by slave labor played a significant role in funding the Industrial Revolution both in the United States and England. The wealth amassed from slave labor created a class of elites and funded their education. The economic effects of slavery are so profound, one could argue that almost every institution in the United States continues to carry its legacy.

America's Cash Crop
Of the crops cultivated in the United States by slaves in the 1800s, none compare to the economic impact made by cotton. Cotton was the leading American export from 1803 to 1937. Look in your closet, then around your home. Take note of all the cotton fabrics. Go to any department store and notice the broad array of

products containing cotton. You can imagine how revolutionary the introduction of cotton was to the world. Cotton's retail popularity created a massive opportunity for marketing companies. And the more promotion that marketing companies gave cotton products, the more the market grew. By the 1820s, cotton was the world's most traded commodity, and the US controlled 80% of it. The amount of cotton produced in the US grew from 20 million pounds in 1805 to over two billion pounds in 1860. While the number of enslaved Africans in the South grew from 50 thousand to 4 million - producing two-thirds of the world's cotton.

This large-scale production of cotton led to new innovations, new businesses, an increase in jobs, and played a fundamental role in funding the Industrial Revolution both in the United States and England. At the time, Europe relied on cotton-picking slaves in the US for more than 80% of its raw cotton supply. Cotton was grown in the US, then manufactured for retail in England - whose textile mills accounted for 40% of their exports. In his book, *Cotton and Race in the Making of America: The Human Costs of Economic Power*, cultural and economic historian Gene Dattel, explains "one-fifth of England's 22 million people were directly or indirectly involved with cotton textiles."

Cotton's complex system of supply and demand led to various inventions, such as the cotton gin and other textile machines that helped increase productivity. As the demand grew throughout the world, many businesses were started to manage the financing, selling, and transportation of cotton products. Roads, railways, canals, and overseas transportation were forced to improve so that cotton could be quickly transported. Additionally, in the United States, the production of cotton directly expanded the use of coal. Before the "Cotton Boom," coal was only used to power steam engines. After the Cotton Boom, coal was used mainly to produce metal and iron for cotton textile factories. Over just a few decades, cotton grew to become the world's first and most crucial factory-made good - and almost anyone who flocked to the US South to grow it became rich.

When word got out about how lucrative the cotton industry was, White businessmen and their families - from northern states in the US and in Europe, - hurried to the South with dreams of getting rich and living the opulent lifestyle many plantation owners flaunted. Cotton was in high demand all over the world. It was not very difficult for a White businessman to buy or rent land, buy or rent a couple of slaves, secure a contract with an English manufacturing company, then grow their business. The US government was selling land at very low costs and many slaves were available for rent or purchase on credit. The efficiency and effectiveness of cotton-picking slaves quickly led international markets to flood Southern plantation owners with even more credit. Plantation owners would then extend credit to their neighbors - which accelerated the rate at which cotton production grew. Mississippi newspaper, *the Natchez Courier*, reported that in the one year between 1835 and 1836, White residents in Mississippi bought as many as ten thousand slaves on credit, at an average price of one thousand dollars per slave. This credit system directly contributed to a head start in wealth building for many families and institutions in the United States.

Elite Education Afforded by Slave Labor
Fortunes built on the backs of slaves allowed for the creation and education of a class of American elites. The sale of slaves paid for the actual building of many Ivy League universities, and schools received continued support by tuition and donations acquired from the profits of slave labor. Princeton, Brown, Columbia, Georgetown, Harvard, Rutgers, and the University of Virginia are just a few of the many educational institutions that benefited from selling slaves. At Georgetown University, slave profits kept tuition free for students during its first 43 years. According to Princeton, 40% of their student body came from slave states in the years before the Civil War. But selling slaves and receiving money from slave owners was not the only way universities benefited from slavery. Many university leaders also owned slaves themselves.

Princeton's first nine university presidents owned slaves at some point in their lives, many during their tenure as president. At Columbia University, at least half of the university's presidents between 1754 and 1865 owned slaves at some point in their lives. Sojourner Truth, a famous abolitionist and women's rights activist, was born enslaved to the first president of Rutgers University, Jacob Hardenbergh.

The theology and business of slavery were also part of the curriculum at many universities. Columbia University revealed that at least one math problem in a 1760's class asked students to "calculate the profits of three investors in a slave-trading voyage to Guinea." And according to Rutger's "Scarlet and Black" project, "The faculty and curriculum at Rutgers, and other early American colleges, reinforced the theological and scientific racism that provided the ideological and spiritual justification for the free labor of Africans, the absolute power of slave owners, and the separation of the races."

At the time, slavery was a normal part of life - a known source and symbol of prosperity. Wealth amassed in the slave economy afforded a new class of elite children an education that would teach them how to maintain their family's fortune, and how to make decisions that would sustain their legacy and social status for many generations.

Unwilling to Let Go

By the time slaves were emancipated, much of the nation's wealth had already been established. Directly and indirectly, slave labor gave White Americans a head start that could never be matched without intentional effort. Although many White Americans advocated for the abolition of slavery, most White Americans were comfortable with the privileges that whiteness gave them. They were not ready or willing to integrate with people who were previously their servants. They were unwilling to part with their newfound wealth, and reluctant to extend or compete for the American Dream promised to them. Ultimately, this inaction to promote racial healing resulted in continued human rights violations and compounding economic and social inequities.

Three

The Jim Crow Era

In the 21 years between the end of slavery and the beginning of Jim Crow, the fate of African Americans was turbulent. Initially, federal troops were sent to the South to enforce emancipation and other Reconstruction Amendments. But when they were ordered to leave, former Confederates regained control and a string of events exploded into one of the ugliest times in United States' history - the Jim Crow era. During this era, African Americans were routinely subjected to institutionalized humiliation, discrimination, physical violence, and more. Eventually, Black people's perseverance in obtaining a quality education resulted in Congress ending the lawful justification of these acts. Still, the trauma experienced during this time would last for generations.

Progress
Immediately after emancipation, the future seemed optimistic for Black folk. In the early months of 1865, the federal government took action to reunite Southern States into the Union and to protect the freedom of Black people so they could build a new life for themselves. Southern States were required to write new state constitutions recognizing Black people as citizens and federal troops were sent down to enforce emancipation and other Reconstruction Amendments. Sure enough, African Americans quickly began to create their own successful communities. All-Black churches and schools sprung up and thrived - also serving

as Black-empowerment community centers. Literacy rates escalated in Black communities, even surpassing some White communities. Black people began farming for themselves. And skills that were once used on the plantation - in masonry, textiles, barbering, and more - began being utilized in Black-owned businesses.

Additionally, Congress established The Freedmen's Bureau - providing millions of former slaves with free food, healthcare, and assistance with legal affairs. The bureau helped legitimize marriages, reconnect families, and funded over 400 thousand dollars worth of teacher training and establishing Black schools. The bureau also incorporated The Freedman's Savings Bank - which served over 100 thousand newly freed Black Americans with 37 branches in 17 states. In its ten-year lifespan, The Freedman's Savings Bank amassed over 57 million dollars - which would compare to over a billion dollars today - with deposits made from Black entrepreneurs, laborers, and soldiers who fought in the Civil War.

Two years after emancipation, Congress passed the Reconstruction Act of 1867, allowing free Black men the ability to participate in their first national election. The increase in voters helped the anti-slavery Republican Party win by a landslide - electing President Ulysses S. Grant. During the same time, many Black men were elected into office at various levels of government. In 1868, the 14th Amendment was added to the Constitution - affirming that African Americans had the same right to equal protection under the law as every other citizen. This meant they could legally conduct business, travel, own property, make contracts, and even bring someone to trial. In 1869, the 15th Amendment was passed outlawing voter discrimination based on race, color, or previous condition of servitude. Collectively, the 13th, 14th, and 15th Amendments - known as the "Reconstruction Amendments" - granted African Americans the right to fully participate in society. Unfortunately, just because these laws were enacted did not mean they were upheld or enforced.

Regress
African Americans won a few political rounds during the Reconstruction Era, however a strong resistance was brewing. President Grant did his best to fight against racism and leave a legacy of political and civic equality. But his ability to steer America's civil rights vision was overshadowed by his lack of economic leadership. At first glance, the United States' manufacturing capacity and overall economy seemed to be growing rapidly. The increase in factories and manufacturing plants resulted in more jobs for everyone, including African Americans. All-the-while, a bubble was inflating.

As the economy became more global, US farmers and businesses were thrust into competition with other countries and forced to lower their price on exports. Large investments were being made into railroads and other infrastructure without profitable returns. Then Germany stopped using silver as currency, which consequently decreased the value of the US dollar - causing inflation and nationwide panic. During the Finance Panic of 1873 and throughout The Great Depression, banks collapsed, the US stock exchange stopped trading, and unemployment reached a record high - which disproportionately affected African American workers.

Meanwhile, the (White) businessmen managing the Freedman's Savings Bank were using the bank's funds to invest in subprime bonds. They were also outright stealing and giving money away to their friends and colleagues. Infested with corruption and on the verge of bankruptcy, Congress asked Frederick Douglass to serve as the bank's new president. As president, Douglass invested 10 thousand dollars of his own money into the bank to revitalize it and gain the trust of other African Americans. He wanted to encourage them to continue depositing their money so that the bank would not collapse. Unfortunately, the bank was beyond saving. In 1874, Douglass went to Congress and announced that the Freedman's Savings Bank was bankrupt and needed to close. Douglass later wrote in his autobiography, "The fact is... I was married to a corpse. The fine building was there, with its marble counters and black walnut finishings... but the life, which was the money, was gone - and I found that I had been placed there with the hope that by some drugs, some charms, some conjuration, or some mighty magic, I would bring it back." Thousands of African Americans never regained their money when the Freedman's Bank collapsed. And this loss was just one of more to come.

Soon, much of the progress made in the Reconstruction Era would become unrecognizable. In order to solve the dispute of who would win the next presidential election, the infamous Compromise of 1877 was made - in secret - between Democrat and Republican members of Congress. Democrats agreed to stop blocking the win for Republican candidate Rutherford Hayes, as long as Republicans agreed to pull federal troops out of the South when elected. The deal was made, President Hayes was elected, and troops were ordered to retreat. The same party who once fought to end slavery ignored the vulnerability of Black communities and gave former Confederate slave owners, and other White supremacists, the ability to regain control of the South. As a result, land occupied by Black people was violently taken away and Black people were forced into civic subservience.

With federal troops gone, "Black Codes" were reestablished throughout the South to reinforce the dominance of White people. Black Codes were an extension of "Slave Codes" - a set of laws that were applied to slaves, but adapted and utilized to oppress free Black people. While the Reconstruction Amendments technically allowed African Americans certain rights, the Black Codes excluded them from others. For example, the combination of the two granted African Americans access to the courts but denied them the right to testify against White people. African Americans could legally vote, but the Black Codes disenfranchised their right to register. Black Codes also prohibited African Americans from holding public office, serving on juries, owning guns, or participating in state militias. African Americans became ineligible for employment unless they had approval from their previous (White) employer. And "contract laws" would penalize anyone who attempted to leave a job before their wage advance was worked off. Moreover, it was a crime to be vagrant - to be Black and unemployed. Among the worst of laws were Black Codes known as "The Pig Laws," which turned misdemeanors into felonies for African Americans.

Once convicted, Southern States could essentially re-enslave prisoners and rent out their labor to make a profit. Local plantations, lumber camps, factories, coal mines, and railroads paid very low rates for convict labor and were responsible for providing them food and housing. It was a win-win situation for states because it eliminated the cost of imprisoning convicts and quickly became a lucrative stream of income. Still, however profitable convict leasing was for states, it was a horrific violation of human rights for its victims. And Black Americans had practically no legal or political power to fight against it.

At the same time, White supremacist groups were growing larger and more prominent in the South, along with their eagerness to end Black empowerment. This was especially true in the small Louisiana town of Colfax. In the election of 1868, William Calhoun, a White Republican, opened up his plantation as a safe place for over 150 Black men to cast their vote. In that election, Republicans earned 318 votes, and Democrats received a mere 49. Later, a group of White Democrats threw Calhoun's ballot box into the river and arrested him for election fraud. Democrats successfully stole that election and took office. Naturally, Black people realized that if they wanted their votes to count, they would need to work together to protect their votes and the candidates they elected. So when the Republican Party won the gubernatorial election in 1872, a group of over 150 Black people gathered inside the Colfax courthouse to make sure the transfer of power would happen successfully. Soon after their arrival, the group was met by over 300 members of the White League - a popular White supremacist group. The White League launched a cannon inside the courthouse, and those who escaped and surrendered were killed in cold blood. It is estimated that 150 Black men were killed in this massacre. And of the over 300 White perpetrators, only 9 were convicted of conspiracy.

In 1876, the 9 convicted perpetrators of the Colfax massacre brought their case before the Supreme Court, who ruled in their favor. In the notorious case of the United States v. Cruikshank, the Supreme Court ruled that the Bill of Rights did not apply to private groups or state governments. This meant groups such as the White League or KKK could not be punished using the 14th Amendment. Then, in 1883, the US Supreme Court ruled that the Civil Rights Act of 1875 was unconstitutional. This meant the 14th Amendment only prohibited states - not citizens - from discriminating. Thus, businesses such as hotels, restaurants, and railroads were legally allowed to discriminate against Black people and segregate public spaces.

In the face of yet another civil rights setback, African Americans continued to advocate for themselves. In 1892, civil rights groups organized a protest against the segregation of public railroads. Homer Plessy led the demonstration by sitting in the "Whites-only" section on the East Louisiana Railroad passenger train. No one objected to Plessy's arrival because he was "White-passing" - with skin so fair that no one could tell he was mixed with Black. After he sat down, he announced that he was, in fact, "seven-eighths Caucasian and one-eighth African blood." After being arrested for refusing to move to the "Blacks-only" car, Plessy sued the railroad. He argued that labeling him Black just to be able to discriminate against him was unconstitutional. After arguing and losing his case in local and state courts, Plessy's case finally reached the Supreme Court in 1895. After months of deliberation, on May 18, 1896, the Supreme Court ruled that a law which "implies merely a legal distinction" between White people and Black people was not unconstitutional. Segregation would remain perfectly legal, as long as facilities were separate but equal. Alas, "Separate" became the new standard in the United States, especially in the South.

The Supreme Court's decision to allow segregation lasted for around 70 years. This era became known as the Jim Crow era - a period where Black Americans were legally set apart, unequally employed, unequally educated, and denied their constitutional rights. They lived under the constant threat of violence and Black women and girls were routinely raped as a way to break down Black men and disrupt the union of Black families. Furthermore, modern research suggests that the trauma African Americans experienced during this time was coded into their genes and passed down to later generations.

Institutionalized Segregation and Humiliation
The whole nation was paying attention to the Plessy v. Ferguson case. It was the perfect opportunity for the Supreme Court to promote racial healing and set a precedent for all Americans to interpret the Constitution with equal regard for all its citizens. Instead, the ruling divided the country and validated racist instincts to

The Jim Crow Era

structure society through a lens of White supremacy. This decision was a massive blow to The Civil Rights Movement. Homer Plessy's railroad demonstration was orchestrated intentionally to highlight just how trivial and humiliating it was for people to be separated by their race. The case was brought to the Supreme Court with hopes that institutions would have to stop violating the constitutional rights of Black Americans. On the contrary, institutional racism was further empowered by the US government.

For Black people, the "Separate but Equal" ruling intensified everyday forms of humiliation, inequity, and violence. As such, the possibility of engaging with White people in public became terrifying. Many Black people preferred to remain insulated in their own communities. Being in public meant being at perpetual risk of losing one's dignity or even their life. Moreover, White supremacist groups were growing, as was their public visibility. In the years between 1889 and 1899, almost 200 Black people a year were being lynched by White supremacists. Black families, especially women and children, were obligated to either stay indoors or travel in groups if they needed to run an errand, walk to school, or go to work.

As deflating as it was to work in a segregated workplace, African Americans were commonly hired at factories and manufacturing plants when production was back on the rise. In these factories and manufacturing plants, there were separate assembly lines for Black and White employees. Systems were put in place to ensure that if a Black person touched a machinery part, it would never again be handled by a White person. And since "race-mixing" or associating with Black people was considered low-class, this kind of systematic separation was obligated for employers to ensure the dignity of their White employees. Also, systems of segregation served as a constant reminder to Black people that, although they shared a working facility with White people, they were still considered less-capable and less-respectable human beings.

The segregation of transportation was another everyday form of institutionalized humiliation. Even when African Americans could afford a first-class ticket, they would still be required to sit in a less-than-desirable part of the train - a section designated for "Blacks-only." It was expected that Black spaces were held to a lower standard of quality and cleanliness than White spaces. And, if a Black person refused to remain in their designated section, they were punished with a fine or jail time.

In many establishments, segregation escalated into the outright discrimination against Black people. It was common for Black people to travel a mile or more just to find a place with a public Black bathroom. And degrading acts of racist humiliation were not reserved for the South - they also took place in the North. A game called "Hit The Nigger Baby " or "African Dodger" was incredibly popular at public events all over the US from the 1880s through the 1950s. A Black person would be hired to attend White events, just to get hit in the face with balls for their amusement. In November 1935, Iowan newspaper, *Lake Park News*, reported a successful high school carnival as a "thrilling athletic event... after this show, the crowd enjoyed themselves in visiting the various booths or trying to ring a duck's neck in a tank of water, or hit the nigger baby." In July 1948, Indiana newspaper, *The Jackson County Banner,* published a headline that read, "Make this big week your vacation time — Bring the Family — Meet Old Friends — Hit the Nigger Babies — Eat Hot Dogs — Join the Fun!" According to the Jim Crow Museum at Ferris State University, the game may "sound like a common carnival target game, but there was one unsettling part, the game's target was a real live human being - a 'negro' human being." Research shows that a wooden target was used as the Black dodger in some cases. Still, in other cases, actual Black "boys" were used. Back then, most people referred to Black men as "boys," so it is virtually impossible to determine the age of these Black event workers. Nevertheless, the popularity of this humiliating game demonstrates the racist sentiment in America during that time, and the desperation some Black people had for employment.

Unequally Employed
In the aftermath of The Great Depression, newly elected President Roosevelt created a series of financial programs - known as The New Deal - in effort to stabilize the economy and provide immediate relief to people in the workforce. But this New Deal disproportionately benefited White people, while Black people remained unemployed at a rate of 50%.

Black people were not welcome to apply for many positions. For example, even though former slaves overwhelmingly possessed advanced craftsmanship skills, Black men only accounted for about 4% of craftsmen's jobs because no one would hire them. When Black men were hired for jobs, they were routinely overworked and underpaid. And at many factories, Black people were prohibited from operating sophisticated machinery. Lonnie Roland, a worker at Firestone, confessed, "There was an unwritten law that Black people couldn't work high-skilled jobs, couldn't have no top jobs operating no machine." Prohibiting Black people from skilled labor was one way employers could justify paying Black people less than their White counterparts. In his book, *Rising from the Rails, Pullman Porters and the Making of the Black Middle Class*, Larry Tye reveals, "A train porter had the best job in his community, but the worst job on the train." And Black people could forget about aspiring for promotions or raises. They were fortunate enough to keep a job - because not only were they the last ones hired, they were the first fired during layoffs.

After slavery, and continuing into the years post-Great Depression, sharecropping was one of the few jobs consistently available to Black people. Regrettably, most African American sharecroppers were severely exploited - many were rarely paid, if ever. Since plantation owners were no longer able to own slaves, they needed to hire workers to maintain their crops. In the same right, most Black people had farming skills and needed to work. Innocently enough, numerous Black families went back to work on plantations as sharecroppers under the pretense that they would share the profits of their labor with the owner. Plantation owners would give sharecroppers a place to stay and let them use their tools as part of a "wage-advance" agreement - which was to be subtracted from the worker's earnings at the end of the season. The amount of money a sharecropper could expect to make fluctuated by season, but their rental expenses always continued to add up. Plantation owners kept track of their own accounting, making it virtually impossible for sharecropping families to prove their earnings. And by the end of the farming season, families would end up owing the plantation owner - indebted to work another year for free to pay it off.

Sharecroppers' debts were rarely able to be paid off and the isolated location of plantations made it hard for workers to leave. If they attempted to escape, they risked a very high chance of being captured by police. If captured, police would take them to court where they would be found guilty of abandoning their debts, fined with court fees, and returned to their employer with an increased debt. Because of this, sharecropping families found themself in a vicious cycle of work without pay or going to jail for not paying off the debt.

Though most working Black Americans faced discrimination and unequal working conditions, there were still those who sustained employment in their own community. In fact, some communities were entirely owned and operated by Black people. There were Black-owned barbershops and beauty salons, cafes and restaurants, record stores and nightclubs, churches, and even funeral parlors. But self-empowering Black families and successful Black businesses were highly insulting - and intimidating - to neighboring working-class White people. As such, it was not uncommon for an angry White community member to file a complaint and legally shut-down a Black-owned business. Moreover, Black owners and workers existed under constant threat of angry White mobs coming to burn down their businesses, light their homes aflame, or worse.

Rape.
Not only were Black people humiliated by segregation, targeted for criminalization, and given unequal employment opportunities, they were also perpetually subject to rape. In her article, "Gender, Black Feminism, and Black Political Economy," Patricia Hill Collins writes about the increased threat of rape Black women had to

manage in everyday life post-slavery. She explains, "No longer the property of a few White men, African American women and girls became sexually available to all White men." On the surface, White men freely sexually assaulted Black men's sisters, wives, and daughters whenever they wanted to. But at the core, rape was another chance for White men to assert their dominance over Black men - an act of terror to emasculate and undermine them for not being able to protect their families.

In May of 2006, Ruth Thompson Miller conducted a case study on "Legal Segregation: Racial Violence and the Long Term Implications," which included interviews with nearly 100 African Americans who survived the Jim Crow era. When asked about girls getting raped while she was growing up, one participant responded, "There were rapes! If White men see a halfway decent woman, if he wanted her, he went up and just grabbed her and starts doing whatever he wanted to do to her. You know, she would fight, and say no, but he would beat her up, slap her, knock her down, and just, just take her. That was the norm back then for the White man to do. If you just happened to be in an area where they were, it could happen to you. We were basically homebound people, so we didn't get out much... Always 'yes sir/no sir, thank you sir' or whatever... never show any attitude or any animosity, for all that would lead to was either a beating, rape, or killing."

The enormity of this issue is almost ironic considering the innumerable acts of violence committed against Black men for allegedly raping or "inappropriately looking at" White women. In his book, *The Black Image in the White Mind: The Debate on Afro-American Character and Destiny*, historian George M. Fredrickson shares that at the beginning of the twentieth century, many scientific journals, newspapers and even best-selling novels promoted a "black rapist" theory. But records prove Black women and children were much more commonly victims of rape during this time. For example, in 1930, a White police officer killed a 14-year-old Black girl in a New Orleans restaurant because she resisted his attempts to sexually assault her. In 1959, four White male students in the Tallahassee area raped a Black university student at gunpoint. It was reported that they were overheard casually talking about wanting to "go out and get a nigger girl." In Americus, Georgia, in July of 1963, nearly 30 Black girls between the ages of 12 and 15 were arrested while buying movie tickets. They were taken to an old run-down building where they were kept for two months. After their release, it was reported that some of the girls were raped and sodomized, and at least one 12-year-old girl was pregnant. The parents of "The Stolen Girls" were never notified of their arrest, location, physical condition, or the reason the girls were arrested. As i write this, i struggle with the question of including the many headlines littered throughout newspapers such as "White Man Rapes Six-Year-Old Girl" in the *Chicago Defender* or "An 11-Year-Old Child Raped Delivering Clothes" in Pennsylvania's *New Journal and Guide*. Part of me feels compelled to share their stories, to honor their lives and to prove how common this experience was - but my gut tells me not to. i will spare you, the reader, and myself, further trauma. Just know, if you choose to research newspapers from the Jim Crow era, you will unearth many stories about the horrors of what it was to be a Black man, woman, or child in that time - constantly at risk of horrendous disregard for your life. Knowing that at any moment, you or a member of your family could become another headline.

Unequally Educated
African Americans faced many serious life challenges during the Jim Crow era. In the midst of it all, they remained steadfast in their pursuit of quality education. Black schools were severely underfunded, understaffed, and under-supplied. Overall, schools in the South were not among America's best, but the education inequality for Black students was unjustifiable. School buildings rarely had heating or cooling and many had leaking roofs, broken floors, and no glass in the windows. Since Black schools were so sparse, it was common for children to have to travel through one or several neighborhoods to arrive at an overcrowded facility. In most cases, an entire grade would have to be taught in one classroom - while in other cases, one teacher could have children as young as toddlers and as old as eighth-grade students in one class.

Black schools were not given the same amount of public funding as nearby White schools. Consequently, Black teachers received less training and were paid less than White teachers in their same community. There were also restrictions on what materials could be taught to Black students. In his book, *The Miseducation of the Negro*, historian Carter G. Woodson reveals that specific textbooks were produced for Black students for many years. Some states even prohibited the inclusion of the Constitution in fear that Black students would read it and attempt to demand or assert their rights. Woodson explains the phycology behind this saying, "If you can control a man's thinking, you do not have to worry about his actions... If you make a man feel that he is inferior, you do not have to compel him to accept an inferior status, for he will seek it himself." Regardless, Black teachers and students made the best of their learning conditions whenever and however possible.

For Black kids, school was not only a place to learn primary education, it was a place where self-dignity was instilled in them. Teachers were there to uplift students and to teach them to empower themselves. Regrettably, a large portion of Southern Black families lived on rural plantations working as sharecroppers, so it was necessary to pull their children out of school once they were old enough to help work the farm. In other cases, Black children in the South would be pulled out of school by plantation owners who believed Black people did not deserve an education - that the worth of their life extended to physical labor, and it was a waste to educate a brain that society would never use.

Thankfully, all White people did not hold the same anti-education sentiment. By the 1900s, White foundations in the North were sending money down south to help build and improve Black school systems. Notably, The Rosenwald Foundation built nearly 5000 Black schools between 1912 and 1932 - with the guidance of Black educator Booker T. Washington. Even so, of the Black children who attended school, most left by the fourth grade. As a result, college attendance in the Black community was very rare.

When Black people did make it to college, few of them were academically prepared enough to graduate. When Black people did graduate, they graduated with large debts and there were minimal opportunities available to them for work. Corporations and other reputable high-paying jobs rarely hired Black employees - and affirmative action programs did not begin until the late 1960s. Many Black college graduates went on to become clergy, civil servants, and businessmen. Another many were fated to return to the farms where their families were sharecroppers, and would advocate for fair working conditions and accounting of debts. A large number of Black women graduates became the housewives of Black men graduates. The majority of Black college graduates went on to become teachers at all-Black schools. And a very few of the graduates became lawyers that would represent students of all-Black schools in the many discrimination cases brought forth in the Supreme Court case of Brown v. Board of Education.

The Road to Equality
In the Plessy v. Ferguson case, the Supreme Court ruled that segregated facilities must be separate but equal. Still, it was well known that the condition of Black schools were far from equal to White schools. Furthermore, many local school board members were known members of the KKK - making it very challenging for Black teachers and parents to advocate for fair learning conditions. Even so, that did not stop their efforts. As early as the year 1881 and until the year 1954, Black families, teachers, and civil rights advocates worked together to sue school districts for various violations of their constitutional rights.

In 1947, Reverend J.A. DeLaine, an African Methodist Episcopal Church minister and member of the NAACP, approached Clarendon County school officials and requested school buses for the Black children in her community. These children were walking up to eight miles each way to school every day, but her request was denied. School officials responded that Black families were the minority and did not contribute the same amount in taxes - so it was unfair to expect White citizens to pay for Black children's school buses. With the help of the NAACP's Legal Defense Fund, Rev. Delaine and other local community members argued their case all the way to the Supreme Court.

The Jim Crow Era

In 1950, Oliver Brown attempted to enroll his daughter, Linda Brown, into a public elementary school just seven blocks away from where they lived. They were denied admittance because the school was intended for White students only. Alternatively, Linda was forced to walk through a dangerous neighborhood to get to a bus where she sometimes had to wait in the cold and rain to get to the Black school - twenty-one blocks away from where she lived. Together, Brown and the NAACP sued the Topeka school board. Their case was denied but would soon make its way to the Supreme Court.

Later that year, members of the NAACP, and thirteen local parents, sued the Board of Education of Topeka Public Schools because Black schools in the area did not offer the same amount of courses and textbooks as their neighboring White schools. Furthermore, Black elementary schools were fiercely overcrowded because there were only four schools available to Black students, compared to eighteen available to White students.

In 1951, parents in both rural and suburban areas of Delaware developed a case with a Black lawyer named Louis Redding against the Delaware State Board of Education. Together they sued the school district for unequal learning conditions. Not only did their children have to travel sometimes twenty miles to get to school, but the curriculum was incomplete, the schools were overcrowded, and the teachers did not have the same advanced degrees as the teachers who taught at the local White schools.

In Washington DC, 1951, the owner of a local African American barbershop, Gardner Bishop, organized the parents and children in his community to march to the local White high school, Sousa High, and demand admittance. In huge contrast to the run-down facilities they were forced to attend, Sousa High was located in a large, modern building with multiple basketball courts and spacious classrooms. It was undoubtedly big enough to admit many more students. When Sousa High denied their admittance, they joined forces with African American civil rights lawyers Charles Houston and James Narbritt Jr. Together, they sued the District of Columbia, arguing that the city needed to create a high school equal to Sousa High for Black students.

In the Commonwealth of Virginia, 1943, African American students were moved from a two-story building into a smaller building that was still under construction and covered in tar paper. These conditions compelled Barbara Rose Johns to lead her classmates on a ten-day school strike in 1951. During the strike, students walked out of the school. Still, they remained on school grounds to share their stories of inequality and display signs advocating for change. NAACP attorney Oliver Hill picked up their case and argued to federal courts for better school conditions.

The NAACP's Legal Defense Fund - along with Linda's dad, Oliver Brown - and their case against the Board of Education of Topeka finally reached the Supreme Court in 1952 - including all of the other cases mentioned above. Together, they presented a compelling argument to the Supreme Court that separate was not always equal. In fact, separate was inherently unequal because it instilled a general sense of inferiority in Black students and in citizens. After much deliberation, in 1954, the Supreme Court ruled that segregation was indeed unconstitutional. This case marked one of the most significant victories for African Americans since the 13th Amendment. It also laid the groundwork for the Civil Rights Act of 1964, which prohibited discrimination in public spaces, and the Voting Rights Act of 1965, which prohibited discrimination in voting. Although segregation and discrimination were officially outlawed, the trauma endured during this time would remain present for years to come.

Generational Trauma
The horrific realities of being Black in America during the Jim Crow era carried a load of institutionalized humiliation, verbal and physical violence, and the obstruction of liberties granted to all citizens by the Constitution. After emancipation, the onset of Reconstruction was enough to inspire hope for a race of formerly enslaved people. Having to endure painful injustices every day, after expecting the opposite, surely made the realities of "freedom" that much more traumatic. Experts in psychology and neurology have found that experiencing trauma can profoundly affect the brain and body, and even change a person's genetic makeup. The stress of trauma can lead to psychological distress, disease, and immune deficiencies, all of which can be genetically passed down and have a reactive effect on future generations.

Dr. Ruth Thompson-Miller, author of *Jim Crow's Legacy: The Lasting Impact of Segregation*, coined the term "segregation stress syndrome" to define the long term effects experienced by those who lived and suffered through the segregation, intimidation, extreme fear, and stress of potential death during the Jim Crow era. According to Thompson-Miller, segregation stress syndrome is the result of long-lasting racial violence. Unlike post-traumatic stress disorder, or PTSD - which focuses on the experiences of one individual - segregation stress syndrome includes several traumatic events that generate symptoms of stress in African Americans as a collective group. Hearing, witnessing, and/or experiencing a traumatic racial event can all lead to symptoms of segregation stress syndrome. Other triggers include the inability to protect a loved one, having to watch helplessly as they are harmed, and bearing witness to lynchings, death threats, the loss of land, rape, and sexual coercion. Like PTSD, the trauma must have involved a life-threatening event and elicit a response of fear, helplessness, or horror in the exposed individual. In her case study, "Legal Segregation: Racial Violence and the Long Term Implications," she reports that numerous survivors of the Jim Crow era exhibited post-traumatic symptoms throughout their interviews, including denial, anger, fear, rage, anxiety, crying, sweating, and difficulty sleeping.

According to Dr. Thompson-Miller's research, many anxieties present in African American communities today are likely rooted in the trauma faced by their ancestors. Furthermore, frequent exposure to news of police killing Black people without penalty may be a continued source of trauma affecting Black Americans as a collective group. Though research is relatively new on the long-term effects of trauma experienced by African Americans, there has been extensive and comparable research on the intergenerational effects of trauma experienced by Holocaust survivors.

Dr. Rachel Yehuda, psychiatrist and neuroscientist at the Mount Sinai School of Medicine, has spent decades studying traumatic stress and the neurobiology of PTSD concerning Veterans, Holocaust survivors, and other trauma victims. Her previous research uncovered that survivors of the Holocaust had lower levels of cortisol than other Jewish adults around the same age - and survivors experiencing PTSD had even lower levels. Then in 2016, she and her colleagues found that epigenetic processes can alter the expression of a gene without producing changes in the DNA sequence - and can be transmitted to the next generation. When conducting a study on the cortisol levels of the descendants of Holocaust survivors, the data revealed that children of Holocaust survivors also had lower levels of cortisol - especially if their mother had PTSD.

Cortisol is the body's main stress hormone and influences the response to flight or fight situations, as well as the ability to recover. Additionally, cortisol affects the body's blood-sugar levels, metabolism, and immune system.

In parallel, both Holocaust and Jim Crow survivors were subjected to torture, cruel, inhuman, and degrading treatment and punishment. They were made to endure daily instances of unprovoked violence, lynchings, rape, theft, criminalization, and witnessed traumatic events - without protection from the state. Likewise, descendants of both groups have been found more susceptible to symptoms of PTSD - including rage, shame, anger, fear, guilt, anxiety, destruction of masculinity, hyper-masculinity, and more. While these events and symptoms of PTSD are comparable, the Holocaust lasted around four years and the Jim Crow era lasted about 70 years. As such, the evidence of intergenerational effects on cortisol production in Holocaust survivors creates cause to believe that the production of cortisol in African American descendants of Jim Crow survivors could also be impacted - and perhaps cause for health concerns.

In 1896, the Supreme Court announced their "Separate but Equal" ruling which spawned the era of Jim Crow. Then, according to a census count, by 1910, 90% of African American's were still living in the South. This means that the vast majority of African Americans were likely to experience at least 14 years of Jim Crow trauma. For a great many of them, it was time for a change. Over the next 60 years, millions of Black people left the South searching for a better life, taking part in one of the largest migrations in human history.

The Jim Crow Era

Four

Exodus: The Great Migration

Between the mid-1900s and the mid-1970s, millions of working-class Black people left the South in what we now know as "The Great Migration." Before leaving, 90% of Black people in the US lived in the South. They made up 50% of Mississippi and South Carolina's population. And accounted for over 40% of the population in Alabama, Louisiana, Texas, and Georgia. Within just a few decades, that number dropped to less than 30% in each of those states. To this day, the Great Migration is the second largest migration in the history of humankind, with approximately six million participants. Black folk had enough of Jim Crow, and for the first time in American history, they could choose their own destiny. They moved to the North and West seeking refuge and opportunities for a better life. In her book, *The Warmth of Other Suns: The Epic Story of America's Great Migration*, Isabel Wilkerson notes, "They were seeking political asylum within the borders of their own country, not unlike refugees in other parts of the world fleeing famine, war, and pestilence."

In many ways, exiting the South greatly improved the quality of life for African Americans. In other ways, it marked the beginning of a new challenge - the challenge of integrating into historically White communities. Nevertheless, Black people moving out of the South and into the rest of America rocked the nation, leaving a profound and ever-lasting impact on American society.

Exodus: The Great Migration

The Way Out

Black people left the South in three major waves. The exodus began during World War I, around 1916. The second wave was in the 1920s, and the third in the 1960s. The route ahead led to east coast cities like DC, Jersey, New York, Philadelphia, and Boston. Roads to the midwest led to Chicago, Detroit, Cleveland, St. Louis, and Kansas City. And pathways to the west coast led to Los Angeles, Oakland, and Seattle. Whether their tickets were afforded, gifted, or work-sponsored, the first pioneers to chart a path away from the Jim Crow South would become an inspiration for generations to come.

When the United States entered World War I, in 1914, companies in the North were in desperate need of labor workers. Then, in 1916, the popular African American magazine *Chicago Defender* ran an ad for the Pennsylvania Railroad - offering free transportation for African Americans in the South who were willing to work on the railroads. At least 13 thousand Black people traveled north with that offer. The Erie Railroad brought another 9 thousand, while the B&O railroad brought about 10 thousand to Baltimore, Philly, Pittsburgh, and Cincinnati. Upon arrival, these new-to-the-North Black folk were met by Black churches, YMCAs, and other community leaders with food, shelter, and guidance about local and social life. Their new industrial and manufacturing jobs paid wages higher than practically any other job in the South. Additionally, they were now allowed to exercise their right to vote, purchase homes, access better schools, and significantly reduced their risk for day-to-day violence. As this generation proved life in the North could be successful, people began to send for their children and family members. By 1920, Philadelphia alone went from a population of 84 thousand African Americans to 134 thousand. In total, about one million African Americans left the South during this time.

As word spread about a better life up north, the second wave of African Americans made their way out of the South during the late 1920s, through the 1940s. This time around, about 2.5 million African Americans arrived on the east coast, midwest, and west coast looking for work.

With the Black population increasing around the nation, political power began to shift, and African Americans began to achieve significant advancements in civil rights. After the back-to-back wins of Brown v. Board of Education (which outlawed segregation) and the Civil Rights Act of 1964 (which outlawed discrimination), another 2.5 million African Americans left the South hoping to arrive in a city where these laws would actually be enforced. Gradually, African Americans began to enhance their quality of life. More Black people became educated. Jobs in every sector became more integrated. And overall, the freedom to be themselves and tell their stories led to new expressions of art that continue to influence American culture.

A New America

In every city they went to, Black Americans reshaped the social, economic, and political environment. They opened new churches, businesses, newspapers and created new communities. To this day, historically Black neighborhoods and institutions, that were created during this era, can be found in almost every major US city. Additionally, the Great Migration is responsible for the cultural advancements during the Harlem Renaissance, and the birth of the Black middle class - who continue to contribute significantly to consumer spending in every category.

The Harlem Renaissance was an important era in American culture. During this time, the intellect and overall capability of Black people were unveiled to mainstream America. Beginning in about 1918 and lasting through the 1930s, Africans from all over the diaspora - the US South, the US North, and the Caribbean - met up in Harlem. Harlem served as a mecca for Black people to come and be free in their skin, celebrate their history, and express their experiences through various outlets. At the time, it was known as "The New Negro Movement" - a radical movement for Black people to create their own narratives and define, for themselves, what it meant to be modern and Black in America. Musicians who migrated from the South brought jazz, blues, and negro spirituals, giving the genres a global platform and opportunity to develop into a mainstream sound. Musicians of the Harlem Renaissance era included Billie Holiday, Louis Armstrong, Duke Ellington, and many more who would pave the way for future generations. African American literature was another important contribution to this era. Black authors rebelled against traditional writing standards and began to discover what their own voices sounded like. They were able to re-write and articulate a new narrative of the Black experience. Not only did they share stories of their past experiences, but they also began to explore what a future could look like. Additionally, writers of the Harlem Renaissance examined very profound philosophies about the human condition and the effects of colonialism.

The popularity of these concepts, delivered by art, contributed to the enlightenment of African Americans all over the nation. Furthermore, Black people in Harlem created their own theaters and films, in which roles were cast using their own people. Although most of these films would only be seen by other Black people, this was the first time in history that African Americans were able to see themselves in leading roles that did not depict them as servants, prisoners, and degenerates. Being immersed in a community where they were no longer the minority allowed Black people in Harlem the freedom to explore themself and their imagination outside the constructs of race and politics. This era was vital because it reimagined what life could be for Black people throughout the United States. This era gave birth to a new version of the American Dream - and ultimately redefined the American Dream for all citizens and immigrants of color.

The Cold Shoulder

While Black people in Harlem were trailblazing the evolution of American culture, Black people in cities throughout the North and West-coast were carving a path of upward mobility in work and social life. Every week, more and more African Americans left the South and began arriving into cities by the hundreds. Cities were getting more populated, and Black neighborhoods were becoming fiercely overcrowded. Many working-class Black people lived together, sharing a room and even a bed - in which day and night shift workers would rotate. Many working-class White men were at war for 10 of the 31 years between 1914 and 1945. For Black men, this meant more job opportunities and less competition. The more they were able to work, the more money they made, and the Black middle class began to thrive.

As cities grew more dense, middle-class Black families started looking outside the city for nicer areas to live - areas with less crime and better school districts. They had the money and were ready to spend it. Still, various forms of institutionalized discrimination made it nearly impossible for Black communities to expand. In and around major cities, many neighborhoods enforced racial covenants that prohibited owners and realtors from selling or renting to Black people. Moving too far from the city was pretty much out of the question because of the risky commute to work. All across the country, there were cities known as "sundown towns," which would expressly forbid Black people from being there past sundown. These towns typically displayed a sign at the city limits, warning, "Nigger, Don't Let The Sun Go Down On You In [Our Town]." James W. Lowen, author of *Sundown Towns: A Hidden Dimension of American Racism*, shared his surprise when researching the topic, saying, "I expected to find about 10 sundown towns in Illinois, my home state, and perhaps 50 across the country. Instead, I have found about 507 in Illinois and thousands across the United States."

Furthermore, some areas prohibited Black people from entering altogether. For example, the entire state of Oregon enforced Black exclusion laws until 1926. Even though White Americans outside of the South were generally more liberal when it came to civil rights for Black people, a great many of them were still uninterested in integration. Throughout history, racial competition in the workplace had been the cause of job instability and social unrest for African Americans. Black labor was cheap labor for employers, so when White soldiers were at war it was not very difficult for a Black man to find labor-work. But when the soldiers returned and demanded their jobs back, Black people were fired in bulk or demoted to the lowest paying and most dangerous positions. Additionally, Black people were not allowed into unions and were sometimes hired as strike-breakers, adding further racial tension. Animosity for the presence of Black folk bled outside of the workforce and into civic society. White people already resented working with Black people and certainly did not want to live among them.

In 1954 - when the Supreme Court ruled that segregation was, in fact, unconstitutional - African Americans finally had the political leverage they needed to begin integrating into White neighborhoods and schools. Expectantly, this too presented racially charged challenges. Every step of the way, Black homebuyers were met with state-sanctioned policies, like redlining, designed to maintain racial exclusivity. Isabel Wilkerson acknowledges these policies as "the pillars of a residential caste system in the North, that calcified segregation and wealth inequality over generations." The majority of White homeowners believed that the presence of Black people would decrease the value of their homes. It was also a huge concern that if Black and White children were integrated at school, they would begin to date each other. So when Black people began moving into more affluent, White neighborhoods, White people fled to exclusively White suburbs. And despite threats of violence, Black people eventually began integrating the suburbs as well. Both in the workplace and society, African Americans remained persistent in taking radical action toward upward social and economic mobility - even at the risk of their lives.

Exodus: The Great Migration

Five

Genocide

Since African Americans arrived in the United States, there have been intentional efforts to extinguish their culture, inflict bodily harm, and outright kill them off. These acts of violence were condoned by law, primarily unpunished in the judicial system, and have even included the participation of law enforcement. The United Nations defines genocide as any of the following acts committed with the intent to destroy, in whole or in part, a national, ethnical, racial, or religious group such as: forcibly transferring children of the group to another group; deliberately calculating conditions of life to bring about its physical destruction; causing serious bodily or mental harm; killing members of the group; and imposing measures to prevent births within the groups. Throughout US history, acts of genocide have been committed against African Americans in every way defined - by both the US government and White American citizens.

Transferring, Colonizing and Erasing Culture
Today, many African American's struggle with identifying their ancestry because unique family history and specific native cultural practices were lost during transference and colonization during slavery. There was little to no respect for enslaved families. They were separated in practical business transactions - traded, gambled away, and sold. Slave marriages were unrecognized and it was common

for slave owners to "breed" their slaves, forcing their strongest men and women to have sex and reproduce. Families were routinely broken up as a way to weaken morale and avoid revolts. And overall, this transference was deeply destructive to the native culture of African people.

In modern society, much of African American culture is rooted in adaptive survival techniques adopted post-arrival. For example, popular "soul food" dishes are inspired by the dishes, made of scraps, that slaves prepared for themselves on plantations. The English language, and even Christianity, were primarily learned on the plantation - where a new, White-led culture was forced upon them. Brought over from various parts of West Africa, all slaves did not speak the same language. So splitting up families made it very difficult for native African languages and cultural practices to survive. Furthermore, it was forbidden for slaves to speak any other language than English.

Since slaves were not allowed to read or write, many slave owners would read the Bible to them and permitted, or required, them to attend Sunday School. "For the slave-holding class, the Bible was very important for them as a warrant for what they understood to be their right to own slaves, to own people. And they preached it that way - that the Bible says they were to be slaves, they were to be obedient slaves, and that was God's will." Allen Dwight Callahan, author of *The Talking Book: African Americans and the Bible*, shares that "there are passages in the Bible that suggest... 'slaves be obedient to your masters'. And [slave owners] knew that those are the passages slaves in the South would hear over and over and over again. And so he thought it would be better for them not to have that book at all." Even so, many stories in the Bible provided slaves with hope and comfort, and they shared those stories through song - creating what we now know as "Negro Spirituals." Practicing any other religion was forbidden. But practicing Christianity was rewarded and could even compel slave owners to treat them with kindness and compassion. Therefore, slaves were incentivized to practice Christianity. It became universally adopted by enslaved Africans across the South - resulting in generations of African Americans who will never know the original religious practices of their ancestors.

Overall, the White-washing of African culture was an intentional method used to disempower and control enslaved people. When the founder of The Whitney Plantation Museum, John Cummins, learned the history of slave colonization, he had this to say, "I had no idea what a commodity they were and how they were treated as a commodity. I had no idea of how deprived they were… not by force of circumstance but by deliberate planning." Deliberate indeed, even after the emancipation of slaves, White people would continue to take it upon themselves to deliberately bring about the physical destruction of Black people.

Public Lynchings
During slavery, the act of lynching was used on plantations to intimidate slaves into subservience and reinforce a racial hierarchy. When slavery ended, lynching continued to be used for the same reasons. Many Southern White people were offended by the audacity of Black people - living freely among them and exercising their right to freedom of speech. Consequently, Black people were lynched for all kinds of allegations. There are reported lynchings of Black people who were accused of contesting a White person, or "calling them a liar." There are cases where Black men would be lynched for allegedly looking at a White woman or raping a White woman. Cases of lynchings were reported for unproven murder accusations, and if a Black man were accused of killing someone and could not be found, his wife would be lynched. Additionally, lynching cases were reported for simply being the wrong color, in the wrong town, during the wrong time of day.

The vast majority of lynchings were never punished. According to the Equal Justice Initiative, only 1% of all lynchings committed after 1900 resulted in someone actually committing a crime. Not only did law enforcement approve these lynchings, often, there were dozens or even hundreds of people involved. One example was in 1921 when the *Memphis Press* wrote a story headlined "Kill Negro By The Inches." The article tells the story of a Black man named Henry Lowery who was lynched and burned for killing, White planter, O.T. Craig and his daughter. Lowery was a tenant farmer and wanted to dispute a matter of payment with Craig. Interrupting Craig's family dinner, Lowery demanded a settlement. Craig was furious at the interruption and refused. As Lowery was backing off the porch, Craig's son shot him, wounding him slightly. Lowery shot back, killing Craig and his daughter. His punishment - public execution. In perverted detail, the *Memphis Press* writer reported the lynching as having 500 spectators who watched, "even after the flesh dropped away from his legs and the flames were leaping toward his face." At the time, claiming "self-defense" against a White person was itself a crime. To this day, there is hardly any evidence of White people being convicted of lynching. If a lyncher was tried and convicted, it was for arson, rioting, or some other minor offense.

When three of her young Black businessmen friends were abducted and lynched, African American journalist, Ida B. Wells, picked up the cause and went to courageous lengths to document the horrors of lynching. She collected extensive data that is still referenced to this day. Not only did she document these happenings, she also advocated for the end of lynching practices - leading both boycotts and protests nationwide. Challenging the racial hierarchy put a target on her back, and in 1892 the office of her newspaper, *The Free Speech*, was burned down by a mob of White protestors. Still, that did not stop her from spreading her message. While speaking at the National Negro Conference in 1909, Wells began by outlining the three major points of her research. "First, lynching is color-lined murder. Second, crimes against [White] women are the excuse, not the cause. Third, [lynching] is a national crime and requires a national remedy."

The Tuskegee Institute, now known as Tuskegee University, began recording lynchings in 1882. Since they began, 1952 was the first year that no lynchings were reported. Then, in 1955, 14-year-old Emmett Till was brutally tortured, lynched, and his body was thrown into a river because a White woman, named Carolyn Bryant, accused him of grabbing her and whistling at her in a grocery store. Emmett's mother fought against a quick burial so that her son's mutilated body could be viewed and photographed. She wanted to, quote, "let the people see what they did to my boy." Emmett's murderers went to trial and were found not guilty. A year after their acquittal, they confessed to the murder in an interview with *Look Magazine*. The murder of Emmet Till caused a worldwide uproar about the ongoing and unpunished murder of Black men. Not only were their murderers left unpunished, so were their accusers. In 2017, Carolyn Bryant confessed that she fabricated her testimony against Emmett Till. She, too, never received any punishment.

Every year since at least 1900, anti-lynching legislation has been proposed to, and ignored by, the United States Congress. In fact, between 1890 and 1952, seven US presidents petitioned Congress to end lynching, and still, they refused. Then finally, in February of 2020, Congress passed the Emmett Till Anti Lynching Act, which established the act of lynching as a civil rights offense and hate-crime subject to criminal penalties. Nevertheless, in the same year - amid global protest against the ongoing and unpunished murder of Black men by police - there were several reported instances of Black men being lynched across the United States. In June of 2020, there were three lynchings reported in just one week. Nooses continue to appear in communities, serving as symbols of intimidation - proving that America's fetish for "Black fruit, hanging from the poplar trees" is still very much alive in some communities.

Killed by Law Enforcement

Since slavery, Black people have been deemed dangerous and subject to the mercy of any trigger-happy racist who sees them as a threat. Throughout history, law enforcement officers have remained at the forefront of genocide against African Americans. Less than 30 years after slavery ended, Black people accounted for over 50% of the people killed each year by police. Fast forward to 2020, Black people still made up 28% of all people killed by the police - while never totaling over 13% of the entire US population. A study in 2019, conducted by researchers at Rutgers University, found that 1 in every 1000 African American males die at the hands of police. "That's better odds of being killed by police than you have of winning a lot of scratch-off lottery games!" declared Rutgers sociologist and leader of the study, Frank Edwards. In addition, their research found that between 2013 and 2015, police brutality was the seventh leading cause of death for Black men between the ages of 25 and 29. The majority of these murders happen in public, and are reminders of the public lynching of Black men that frequently occurred in the early 1900s.

On August 9th, 2014, 18-year-old Michael Brown Jr. and his friend were walking down their neighborhood street when they were racially profiled - mistaken as robbery suspects - and questioned by a police officer in Ferguson, Missouri. After a struggle in the police car, two shots were fired from the police officer's gun. Michael and his friend took off running, and the officer began shooting in their direction. Many of the case details are unclear, but here is what we know: Michael was facing the police with his hands above his head, in surrender position, when he was shot at least six times from a distance. Before being covered, his body laid faced-down in a pool of blood - in the middle of the street for the entire neighborhood to see - for four hours. The officer was never indicted for killing Michael Brown Jr. And though his murder ignited protest around the world - against the ongoing and unpunished murder of Black men - this was just another state-sanctioned public execution of a Black man in America. Another lifeless body in the street, serving as a reminder of how much the United States devalues Black life and what could happen when a Black man steps out of line.

Comparable to lynching, the majority of police who kill people go unpunished. In 2015, Mapping Police Violence was created by a research collective that began compiling comprehensive data on police killings nationwide - something no government agency has ever done. Their data reveals that, of all the people killed by police from 2013 to 2020, 98% of officers were not charged with any crime.

The Civil War Draft Riots of 1863 - Manhattan, NY
In March of 1863, the Civil War draft went into effect - which predominantly drafted working-class White immigrants. Black people were exempt from the war, and allowed to continue working, since they were not considered citizens. This infuriated White immigrants who traveled to the United States with the understanding that their white skin granted them privileges in society and priority in the workforce. Then, when word spread that wealthy White people could pay just 300 dollars to get out of the draft, the White working-class became enraged. They really did not want to go to war but could not afford the exemption fee. Still, 300 dollars was less than half of the average price to buy a slave. For the draft-exemption fee to be valued at only 300 dollars implied that their lives were worth less than a slave's life.

On July 13th, 1863, the angry mob of White working-class immigrants began rioting throughout Manhattan to declare their outrage about the draft. Though very quickly, their protest about the draft spiraled into a rampage on a mission to eliminate Black people. Over the next three days, the mob brutally attacked any Black people in their path. Black people's homes were burned down, an all-Black orphanage was burned to the ground, and Black businesses were ransacked and destroyed.

About 120 people died in the riot, and most all were Black men. 11 Black people were lynched in the streets - including one man who was first stoned, beaten with clubs, then lynched by a crowd of 400. Thousands of people were injured and property damage was estimated between 1 and 5 billion dollars - which would be valued at around 20 to 100 billion dollars today.

New Orleans Massacre of 1866
After the abolition of slavery, Louisiana ratified a new state Constitution acknowledging the freedom of slaves. Still, it maintained, "we hold this to be a government of White people, made and to be perpetuated for the exclusive benefit of the White race... people of African descent cannot be considered as citizens of the United States."

In 1866, a parade of 130 Black New Orleans residents marched behind the American flag to the Louisiana Constitutional Convention. Their plan was to protest the disenfranchisement of their votes and assert that voting was their constitutional right. On the way there, angry mobs tried to discourage them by picking fights and firing off guns. When they arrived they were allowed inside, only to learn that they were surrounded by police, firemen, and angry White citizens - by order of the mayor. The mob opened fire on the building, shooting into the windows and into the crowd. Delegates that attempted to surrender were killed on the spot and those who attempted to run were chased down and killed - their bodies were spread over several blocks of the convention. Then, what began as a mission to kill the Black delegates, spread into the city where Black people - who were never even at the convention - were shot in the streets, pulled off of streetcars, beaten, and killed.

By the end of the massacre, at least 200 Black Union war veterans were killed, including 40 delegates at the convention. Another 46 were wounded.

The Memphis Massacre of 1866

In 1866, from May 1st to the 3rd, mobs of White men - led by the Memphis police - attacked, robbed, and killed Black soldiers and civilians. They raped Black women. And burned down Black homes and churches - even while people were inside. Eyewitnesses claim that the riots started for no apparent reason. But later investigations suggest the riots were started because working-class White immigrants were angry about having to compete with newly-freed Black people for work, housing, and social space. In his book, *Your Old Father Abe Lincoln Is Dead and Damned,* Kevin Hardwick proposes that the riots were a way for White men in Memphis to "assert their dominance over Black people and attempt to establish limitations on Black behavior."

The reported aftermath was 46 murders, 5 rapes, and 285 people injured. No prosecutions were made.

The Atlanta Race Riots of 1906

In 1906, the combination of job competition, the criminal portrayal of Black people in the media by political candidates, and flat-out racism ignited an angry mob of White people in Atlanta, Georgia. They went on a two-day rampage, from September 22nd to the 24th, shooting Black people at random and destroying their businesses. Hundreds of people were injured, and the Black economy suffered for many years later.

The riot made national headlines, so the actual number of deaths will never be known because corrupt local government and media misrepresented information to "save face" and not give Atlanta a bad name. However, Atlanta's political and media corruption was no secret. Just days later, on September 28th, 1906, *The New York Times* reported, "the sensational manner in which the afternoon newspapers of Atlanta have presented to the people the news of the various criminal acts recently committed in this county, has largely influenced the creation of the spirit animating the mob of last Saturday night; and that the editorial utterances of the Atlanta news, for some time past, have been calculated to create a disregard for the proper administration of the law and to promote the organization of citizens to act outside of the law."

It was reported that 25 people died in this rampage, but later estimates suggest the number of people murdered was closer to 100.

Genocide

Red Summer 1919
On July 27th, 1919, a 17-year-old African American boy named Eugene Williams was swimming with friends in Lake Michigan. While in the water, he crossed over an imaginary barrier which separated the "White" and "Black" park of the beach. A group of White men began throwing stones at him, hit him, and he drowned. When police arrived at the scene, Black eyewitnesses pointed out the White man responsible for the boy's death. Yet the officers refused to make an arrest. As word of the incident spread, angry mobs of both White and Black people gathered on the beach. Eventually, huge fights broke out and continued for an entire week. Shootings, arson, and violent attacks left 23 Black people and 15 White people dead. Over 500 people were reported injured. And an estimated 1000 Black families were left homeless after their homes were set aflame.

Between April and November of 1919, there would be 25 major riots and instances of mob violence throughout the United States. Additionally, there were 97 recorded lynchings and a three-day-long massacre in Elaine, Arkansas - where over 200 Black men, women, and children were killed after Black sharecroppers tried to organize for better working conditions.

Tulsa Massacre of 1921
On May 30th, 1921, in Greenwood, OH, a 19-year-old Black boy named Dick Rowland and a 17-year-old White girl named Sarah Page rode an elevator together. A White clerk working in the building reported to police that she heard Page scream, and when the elevator opened Rowland ran out.

The following morning, Rowland was arrested and taken to the police station. The police were conducting a silent investigation because Page said she was not pressing charges and the whole incident was just a misunderstanding. Rowland would have been released that afternoon, but instead he was transferred to the county jail for his own safety. While in custody, death threats against him were being called into the police station.

Turns out, earlier that day, *The Daily Tribune*, a local White newspaper, published an utterly untrue account of the incident - claiming that Rowland was detained because he "attacked her, scratching her hands and face, tearing her clothes." Rumors spread and grew out of control inciting an angry White mob who planned to destroy the entire Greenwood community - the community referred to as "Little Africa" by *The Daily Tribune,* but we now know as "Black Wall Street."

On June 1st, 1921, Greenwood was looted, burned, and bombed to oblivion. The governor declared martial law, and the National Guard imprisoned over six thousand African Americans. The violence continued for 24 hours.

The aftermath included 35 city blocks burned to the ground. Over 800 people were treated for injuries. Historians believe that as many as 300 people died in the massacre.

1967 Detroit Riots
On July 23rd, 1967, at 3:15 AM, the Detroit police raided an unlicensed after-hours drinking club during a welcome-home party for two returning Vietnam War veterans. Police arrested everyone in attendance, including 82 African Americans. Local residents witnessing the arrests began to protest - and someone threw a brick into one of the police cars which ignited an explosion of violence.

Racial tensions in the city were already high. This raid was the final straw for a community regularly subjected to unwarranted searches, harassment, excessive use of force, and the unpunished murders of Black men by police. Enough was enough, and people rioted in the streets. On July 25th, the National Guard arrived, and the riot ended on the 27th.

The city burned for 5 days destroying around 2,000 buildings and leaving about 400 families homeless. More than 7,000 people were arrested. Over 1,000 people were injured. And 43 people died. 33 of those who died were Black - and most were killed by the police.

The Tuskegee Syphilis Experiment
In the fall of 1932, fliers began appearing around Macon County, Alabama, promising "colored people" special treatment for "bad blood." The fliers boasted, "Free Blood Test, Free Treatment By County Health Department and Government Doctors," they also included the warning that "YOU MAY FEEL WELL AND STILL HAVE BAD BLOOD. COME AND BRING ALL YOUR FAMILY."

Hundreds of Black men signed up. During their check-ups, 600 men were told they had rheumatism, or "bad stomachs," and that they were eligible to receive free treatment, free meals, free physicals, and free burial insurance. In reality, 399 of those men were diagnosed with syphilis and 201 were used as a control group without the disease. Without their consent, they would all become participants in a research study on untreated syphilis in the Negro male. The Center for Disease Control reported that the program was intended to last only six months, but later, the decision was made to follow the men until death. Local physicians were also asked to assist with the study and agreed not to treat the men.

Eventually, in 1972, whistleblowers brought an end to the experiment. Though, unfortunately, the study had already ruined the lives of its unknowing participants. Not only did participants die from syphilis-related complications, many of their wives and children also contracted the disease.

It is widely believed that the men diagnosed in this experiment were, perhaps, injected with the disease during their initial check-up. Whether that is true or not, this betrayal of the medical industry put African Americans at further risk because it instilled a collective distrust in the medical industry and created apprehension for receiving healthcare. Although, this persisting skepticism about receiving healthcare is understandable. The Tuskegee Experiment was not the only time in US history where the government and medical industry colluded in the genocide of Black people - blatantly lying to those who believed they were being cared for.

Unauthorized Sterilizations
In the early 1900s, The English Eugenics Movement made its way to the United States - and by 1935, 41 states had laws, or pending laws, allowing eugenics programs. During this time, many women went to the doctor for routine medical procedures and left sterilized without their consent - unable to ever have children.

In contrast to the English - who focused on selective breeding for positive traits - the US focused on breeding out negative traits. Initially, "negative traits" pertained to poor people of all races - but women of color eventually became the majority of those targeted for these procedures. For example, in North Carolina, by 1954 black girls accounted for 23% of all sterilizations - shooting up to 60% by the late 1960s.

The effects of a racial caste system were used to justify these sterilizations. Many uneducated women of color were diagnosed as "feeble-minded" and tricked into signing a waiver for sterilization, when being told a different procedure was taking place. In her book, *Choice and Coercion: Birth Control, Sterilization, and Abortion in Public Health Welfare*, Johanna Schoen quoted social worker, Elise Davis, saying, "The expectation was that Black people were not able to take care of themselves. They were all illiterate and retarded." Countless amounts of young Black women were coerced into agreement and told that their welfare benefits would be taken away if they did not agree to the procedure. And many rape victims - who gave birth as a result of the rape - were sterilized afterward without their consent. Moreover, most sterilizations were conducted on young women under the age of 26 - and a large portion were performed on minors under the age of 18.

Genocide committed against Black Americans, and the apathy developed when constantly being exposed to their visible suffering, are both lingering consequences of the inaction taken to promote racial healing immediately after slavery. Furthermore, the effects of transference, separations, public executions, and medical violence still live on in modern society. Black people are rewarded and praised when they can assimilate to White standards of education and personal presentation. The vast majority of police that kill Black men go unpunished. Public executions by police continue to mirror the public lynchings of the past - implying an institutional lack of value for Black life. And although laws permitting sterilizations have been repealed, Black women across the nation still struggle for fair and safe reproductive care. In 2018, the infant mortality rate for "Black, non-Hispanic" women peaked at a rate of 10.8 per 1000 births. Furthermore, Black mothers are two to six times more likely to die during childbirth than White mothers. Black people are more likely to experience anxiety and apprehension about getting vaccines and other medical treatments. And even in the news media and Hollywood, the death and suffering of Black people is disproportionately more visible than the death and suffering of White people. Sorry not sorry, but now that it has been pointed out to you, it will be hard not to see it.

Genocide

Six

Evolved Slavery: The US Criminal Justice System

The free labor of enslaved Black people was the most impactful resource that allowed the United States to become one of the largest economies in the world. When slaves were finally freed from the plantation, Black people were targeted and rapidly incarcerated in high volume - then rented out as cheap labor for businesses. Prisoners were leased by courthouses and jails to local companies for a fee that would turn a profit and pay everyone who worked there. The opportunities created from imprisoning people continued to grow into our modern criminal justice system. Today, the United States' criminal justice system incarcerates more people than any other country in the world and is the number one employer in the United States - surpassing both Walmart and Amazon combined. A report by the cites that, in 2012, the more than 2.4 million people who worked for the criminal justice system made up 1.6% of the entire US workforce, not including the prisoners themself or the employees of the contracted companies that provide supplies and services. Unfortunately, Black lives disproportionately remain the target market that fuels this multi-billion dollar industry.

Evolved Slavery: The US Criminal Justice System

The Infamous Exception
Freedom from slavery lasted a very short time for many Black people in the United States. In 1865, Congress passed the 13th Amendment declaring that neither slavery nor involuntary servitude shall exist within the US - except as a punishment for a crime. Ever since this infamous exception has been exploited and used as a loophole to maintain a free-labor market and grow a thriving industry rooted in incarceration.

Mass Incarceration
Black people were freed from slavery in 1865, but by the 1870s, Black people made up 95% of the Southern prison population and have disproportionately filled prisons ever since. Fast forward 130 years, and still, in the year 2000, the US Census reported that while Black people only made up 19% of the entire southern population, they accounted for 54% of the southern prison population. In fact, it was reported that Black people were overrepresented in prisons in every state and US territory. And as of January 2021, the Federal Bureau of Prisons reported that African Americans account for 38% of inmates nationwide, despite accounting for only around 12% of the country's entire population.

For many years, Southern States rejected the idea of freeing slaves because it would collapse their business model, which relied heavily on free labor. Even New York considered emancipating when southern states seceded from the Union because so much of their wealth was connected to the slave economy. Once slavery ended, the Southern economy was doomed. Many farmers survived by swindling Black people into working for free under the guise of sharecropping. But in 1868, when Black people were granted full American citizenship, White people in the South faced being politically outnumbered. To disenfranchise the Black vote, a culture of fearing Black people was strategically created and promoted. Black people were depicted in the media to be angry, violent, and untamed. Politicians would reinforce people's race-based fears and campaign with a promise of cleaning up the streets. Meanwhile, Black people were increasingly victimized by unfair and false accusations.

150 years later, society continues to perpetuate false stigmas about Black people - asserting that they should be feared more than anyone else. In his book, *Breaking Rank: A Top Cop's Exposé of the Dark Side of American Policing*, former police chief Norm Stamper dedicated an entire chapter to "Why White Cops Kill Black Men." He acknowledges that White cops are simply afraid of Black men and this fear is a defining reason for police racism. He shares, "At first I was afraid of everyone, White, Black, old, young. I got over most of these fears pretty quickly… But not, however, my fear of Black men." According to Stamper, this fear is instilled as early as police academy where they learn about the "almost psychotic" hatred some

young Black men have for police officers. "Legitimate 'kill or be killed' events do happen - far more often today than when I was a beat cop." He continues, "A police officer would be a fool not to be vigilant. But I'm afraid this reality has licensed panicky White cops to shoot Black men when they should be talking, or fighting, their way out of a sticky situation."

In places like New York and Chicago, police departments are encouraged to "stop-and-frisk" anyone they think looks suspicious. In New York, about 55% of all stops are Black people, and in Chicago, around 71% of all stops are Black people. In 2015, New York's Mayor Bloomberg was recorded saying, "You want to spend the money on a lot of cops in the street. Put those cops where the crime is, which means minority neighborhoods. One of the Unintended consequences is, people say, 'Oh my God, you're arresting kids for marijuana that are all minorities.' Yes, that's true. Why? Because we put all the cops in minority neighborhoods… because that's where all the crime is. And the way you get the guns out of the kid's hands is to throw them up against the wall and frisk them." Of the five million reported stops in New York City during his terms as mayor, 96% of them were reported completely innocent. Although racial profiling remains the most consistent factor in the over policing of Black communities, there are several other notable contributions to the state-sanctioned mass incarceration of Black people.

Black Codes, Convict Leasing, Peonage, and Jim Crow

Immediately after emancipation, laws intended for slaves, formally known as the "Slave Codes," were edited to apply to newly freed Black people and were enacted as the "Black Codes." These extremely unfair laws, combined with racially-biased judges and juries, deliberately targeted Black people and enhanced their penalties. These laws were enforced intentionally to maintain dominance over Black people, reinforce White-supremacy, and served as a justification to re-enslave Black convicts and profit from their labor. This marked the first surge in the United States' prison population and the eruption of convict leasing. Convict leasing provided prison labor to plantations, developers, railroads, coal mines, private companies, and corporations. Businesses would be required to feed and house the convicts, which lifted the state's financial burden and in turn made them a profit. This system proved to be incredibly successful. Over time, many businesses began to rely heavily on the cheap labor of prison convicts. By 1898, almost 75% of Alabama's entire annual state revenue was made from leasing convicts. Subsequently, the more money states made from leasing convicts, the more money they could invest into hiring law enforcement officers - which increased the number of convicts brought in and leased out.

Evolved Slavery: The US Criminal Justice System

However profitable convict leasing was for states, it was a horrific and gross human rights violation for its victims. Prisoners were chained together, lacked proper food, clothing, and shelter, and became increasingly susceptible to illness. They were abused, overworked, and many died before the end of their sentences. For these businessmen, prisoners were merely used as cheap, disposable labor tools. Unlike with slaves, there was no incentive to treat a prisoner well. The total cost to purchase, feed and house a prisoner was extremely low. Slaves, on the other hand, were expensive but could create new profit by having children and producing more slaves who could work and continue to reproduce for generations. Because of this, slave owners were motivated to take a certain amount of care for their slaves. In contrast, since prisoners were so cheap, businesses could work them as hard as possible and discard them whenever they were physically unusable or dead. In 1873, 25% of all Black convicts leased out died while imprisoned. Eventually, people began to protest against these inhumane conditions, and working-class White Americans were not happy about having to compete with prisoners for jobs. By popular demand, convict leasing was legally "abolished" in 1928; but it still remains in practice today, legally, under the 13th Amendment. Many large manufacturing companies continue to employ prison laborers for pennies on the dollar. And Louisiana's infamous prison, Angola, continues to require prisoners to "work the field," harvesting crops in the presence of armed guards - very much aware that their forced labor is an extension of that which their ancestors were forced to do.

Another tactic used to entrap Black people into forced labor was called peonage - also known as "debt slavery" or "debt servitude." Through peonage, employers could force employees to pay off a debt by working for them. Although Congress outlawed peonage in the Anti-Peonage Law of 1867, historian Antoinette Harrell discovered many cases of peonage slavery alive in the South as late as the 1960s. Because they lived in rural areas, they were able to keep their slaves from ever learning about their rights. In other cases, Southerners could justify keeping peonage slaves by exploiting "the exception" of the 13th Amendment. Black people would be convicted and found guilty - of an actual or wholly made up petty crime - then fined for both the crime and additional court costs. If and when they were unable to pay the fines, a local businessman would step forward to pay the fine for them. In exchange, the convicted person would have to sign a contract agreeing to work for the businessman without pay until the debt was paid off. Other times a judge would never even have to convict the person accused. All they needed to do was threaten to send the defendant to a far-away labor camp unless they accepted a plea deal - which back then was called a "confess judgment." In this case, a local businessman would step forward to act as a "surety" - vouching for the character of the accused and offering the court a bond, which the judge would accept without ever giving a verdict. Again, the defendant would have to sign a contract agreeing to work without pay until the surety of the bond was paid off. Because Black men were being targeted so fiercely, they would practically have to be lucky, or subject themself to humiliating subservience to White people in their community, if they were going to avoid falling victim to this system.

In 1877, Congress voted to legalize segregation, and even harsher "Jim Crow" laws replaced the Black Codes - igniting the second major surge in prison populations. During this period, the prison population grew from 112 thousand in the 1910s to 332 thousand in the 1960s. When and if a prisoner was released, they were unable to vote or get a job. And if a Black man were caught in the street without a job, they were considered vagrant - and vagrancy was a crime punishable by jail time. These laws were intentionally created and enforced to increase the likelihood of an ex-con returning to prison. Thus, effectively creating a criminal class of Black people.

The War on Drugs Pt 1 - Nixon

In 1971, President Nixon launched the United States' first War On Drugs, declaring drug abuse as "public enemy number one in the United States." As a result, federal funding for drug control agencies increased, mandatory minimum sentences were introduced, and the Drug Enforcement Agency (also known as the DEA) was created. During this period, the prison population grew from 357 thousand in 1970 to 513 thousand in 1980. Mandatory minimums significantly contributed to this prison boom because they guaranteed prison time for any drug offense. Although, the real offense was that Black communities were policed and punished much more harshly than drug offenders in White communities. Nevertheless, Nixon's war on drugs laid the foundation for the next several decades of mass incarceration in the United States.

In a 1994 interview with Dan Baum - a Harper's Bazaar journalist - John Ehrlichman, the domestic policy chief of Nixon's administration, confessed, "You want to know what this was really all about? The Nixon campaign in 1968, and the Nixon White House after that, had two enemies: the antiwar left and Black people. You understand what I'm saying? We knew we couldn't make it illegal to be either against the war or Black, but by getting the public to associate the hippies with marijuana and Blacks with heroin and then criminalizing both heavily, we could disrupt those communities. We could arrest their leaders, raid their homes, break up their meetings, and vilify them night after night on the evening news. Did we know we were lying about the drugs? Of course, we did."

The War on Drugs Pt 2 - Reagan

In 1982, President Ronald Reagan double-downed on Nixon's legacy by announcing his own War On Drugs. During his presidency he increased penalties and set standardized sentences for the Use and sale of drugs with the Comprehensive Crime Control Act and the Anti-Drug Abuse Act. Even for a first-time non-violent drug charge, these Acts could guarantee 5 to 40-year sentences and even life in prison.

In the 1980s, the Use of cocaine was an epidemic in the United States. Powder-cocaine was prevalent in more affluent White communities, while crack-cocaine was popular in poorer Black communities. If caught with the drug, the Reagan administration made it a point to set the harshest penalties for crack. For example, a possession conviction of five grams of crack-cocaine guaranteed a minimum sentence of five years in prison, while it would take a possession conviction of 500 grams of powder-cocaine for the same five year sentence. This in particular, was a blatant announcement to America that this "War On Drugs" was, in fact, an intentional effort to imprison Black people.

During Reagan's eight-year presidency, the prison population doubled, increasing from 518 thousand to 1.1 million. African Americans accounted for 53% of the nation's inmates, while only totaling 13% of the entire population.

Crime Bill Clinton

After 16 years of Republicans in office, and gang violence on the rise, Democratic nominee Bill Clinton, won the nation's vote in 1993 while promising to remain "tough on crime." Almost immediately, he passed the largest crime bill in US history - The Violent Crime Control and Law Enforcement Act, also known as "The 1994 Crime Bill." This bill put the MASS in mass incarceration. It provided the country with 100 thousand new police and invested 9.7 billion dollars into creating new prisons. It enforced mandatory minimums and expanded death penalty-eligible offenses. It also dedicated 6.1 billion dollars to prevention programs, "designed with the significant input of experienced police officers," which proved to focus more on punishment rather than prevention or rehabilitation. The consequences of these initiatives would remain in effect for well over a decade, and contributed to the Unjust incarceration and separation of many families. In fact, by the year 2016, inmates sentenced with mandatory minimums still made up 55% of the US prison population.

During Bill Clinton's presidency, the prison population doubled again, increasing from 1.1 million in 1990 to over 2 million in 2000. By this time, Black people accounted for 43% of incarcerations while only totaling 12% of the entire US population. And though the "tough on crime" sentiment was aimed at reducing gang violence, the majority of inmates were incarcerated for non-violent drug offenses.

Bail, Plea Bargains, and the Money Made

In 2020, the Prison Policy Initiative reported that 65% of the United States' jail inmates have not been convicted of any crime. That number jumps to 74% when you include people held in local jails that rent out space to other agencies like ICE, State Prisons, and the US Marshals. A small percentage of these people will actually be convicted and go to prison. Most of them are in jail simply because they were charged with a crime and cannot afford bail.

Bail is the punishment given whether you committed a crime or not. When a person is arrested, a judge decides if that person will be released before trial and the amount of bail that person will have to pay to be released. There is absolutely no requirement for a judge to set bail in order to release a person pre-trial. Moreover, the Constitution forbids a person to be imprisoned for not paying a debt. In the movies, it is common to see bail being associated with the likelihood of a person being a flight risk or danger to society. However, in real life, two-thirds of pre-trial inmates are charged with non-violent petty crimes. Over-policing in poor Black communities results in poor Black people being disproportionately held in jail pre-trial because they cannot afford to pay for their release. Meanwhile, the bail bondsman industry makes over 1.4 billion dollars a year granting high-interest loans, and insurance companies make about 2 billion dollars securing those loans.

People who are held in jail before trial are more likely to lose their jobs, custody of their children, and be convicted of the crime after agreeing to a plea bargain. The longer a person is held in jail, the more their life on the outside falls apart, and the more susceptible they become to accepting an unjust or untrue plea bargain just to get out. In 2017, about 94% of everyone in prison accepted a plea bargain at the state level and around 97% at the federal level. When standardized sentencing went into effect, the nation saw a boom in the amount of felony charges, which consequently led to a boom in the amount of people required to pay bail - and a boom in the amount of people who continue to accept plea bargains.

People are getting locked up by the thousands, and it is difficult for local courthouses and attorneys to process everyone. As a result, judges and public defenders are overworked and do not have enough resources to send everyone to trial. In most cases, judges and public defenders compel inmates to take plea deals - even when the inmate claims to be innocent - telling them that they will not have to go to trial and risk facing harsher penalties if convicted. As outrageous as it sounds, this is the current reality of the US justice system.

The tragedy of Kalief Browder is one example of how this justice system is failing big time. In New York City, on May 15th, 2010, 16-year-old Kalief and his friend were on their way home from a party when they were stopped by police for fitting the profile of robbery suspects. The 9-1-1 caller, Roberto Bautista, was at the scene and identified them as the Black guys that robbed him of his backpack containing a $700 camera, a credit card, and an iPod touch. The police searched the boys and did not find a weapon, backpack, or any of the items. Bautista changed his story several times. He initially suggested the robbery happened the night of the 9-1-1 call, then he said it happened two weeks earlier on May 2nd, then he changed the date again to May 8th. After further questioning at the scene, Bautista implied that the boys had merely tried to rob him, but may not have been successful. Without any evidence, the police arrested Kalief and his friend anyway.

Before he ever went to trial, a judge set Kalief's bail at 10 thousand dollars. His family could not afford to pay that, so Kalief was eventually charged with robbery, grand larceny, and assault. He was sent to await trial at Riker's Island - one of the nation's most notoriously violent prisons. Maintaining his innocence, Kalief was committed to having his case go to trial, even at the risk of being sentenced up to 15 years in prison if found guilty. Kalief and his public defender submitted many requests of readiness, but the prosecution deferred the case for two years. In 2012, Kalief's lawyer offered him a plea deal, 3.5 years in prison if he pleads guilty - Kalief refused. Later that year, the sentence was reduced to 2.5 years, but he refused to plead guilty to a crime he never committed.

During his time in prison, Kalief was routinely bullied by inmates, brutally beaten by prison guards, and encouraged to commit suicide. He spent a total of two years in solitary confinement. On one occasion, after being sent back to prison by a judge, he attempted to slit his wrist. Three years awaiting trial, Kalief pleaded "not-guilty" to eight judges before meeting the final judge that offered him a plea bargain of immediate release and time served, if he pleaded guilty to two misdemeanor charges. Kalief refused the deal. He pleaded "not guilty" and went back to jail for an additional two months before being released with all charges dropped against him - still never having gone to trial.

After being released, Kalief filed a lawsuit against the city and won. He got his GED and tried to reintegrate back into society, but was battling major depression. In a 2014 interview with New Yorker journalist, Jennifer Gonnerman, Kalief revealed, "It's been a year now, and I got a part-time job, and I got my GED. People tell me because I have this case against the city, I'm all right. But I'm not alright. I'm messed up. I know that I might see some money from this case, but that's not going to help me mentally. I'm mentally scarred right now. That's how I feel. Because there are certain things that changed about me and they might not go back... I feel like I was robbed of my happiness." Eventually, he enrolled in a community college where, in May of 2015, he wrote a paper titled "A Closer Look at Solitary Confinement in the United States," explaining the mental health-risk it poses and advocating for reform. In June of 2015, Kalief Browder took his own life. By sharing his story, Kalief shined a spotlight on others like his. He also shined a spotlight on the Unjust bail system and the ramifications of not accepting a plea deal when offered.

Billions of US dollars are made at the expense of incarcerating its citizens. According to a study by The Prison Policy Initiative, released in 2017, each year the prison industry makes the healthcare industry about 12.3 billion dollars; Construction companies make about $5 billion; Food companies receive about $2.1 billion; Utility companies receive about $1.7 billion; Private companies that supply commission goods receive about $1.6 billion; Telephone companies receive about $1.3 billion; and Private prisons profit about 374 million dollars in government stipends. What started as a way to sustain an economy reliant on the free-labor of Black Americans has grown into a 182 billion dollar-a-year industry.

Evolved Slavery: the US Criminal Justice System

Seven

Stunted Growth: Exploring the Racial Wealth Gap

Despite the ongoing racial discrimination and implicit biases encountered on the path to wealth building, African Americans remain resilient in working for economic equality. In 2016, the median net worth of Black households was about 17 thousand dollars, compared to White households with around 171 thousand dollars. The Institute on Assets and Social Policy (IASP) followed American households over 25 years, from 1984 to 2009, studying how both policy and lived experience affect wealth accumulation. Their research found that the fundamental factors contributing to the US racial wealth gap are: unequal access to education, unequal employment opportunities, income inequality, homeownership inequality, and unequal access to financial education. Furthermore, the continuing effort to disenfranchise Black voters suppresses their ability to affect change on a local and national level. Over the last several decades, hardly any progress has been made in reducing racial income and wealth inequalities. This remains true even when wealth holdings grow at a faster rate for Black households than White households. The Corporation for Enterprise Development estimates that it would take about 228 years for the wealth African American households to reach that of White households. This estimate does not include delays in progress due to nationwide economic downturns. To forge a direct path to racial equity in the United States, it is essential to acknowledge the facts and effects of discrimination, and the challenges that navigating racism creates for Black Americans.

Stunted Growth: Exploring the Racial Wealth Gap

Unequally Educated

Having a college degree has proven to increase the amount of wealth Americans are able to accumulate. However, the difference in the amount of wealth between White and Black Americans, post-graduation, is astonishing. On average, White college graduates hold three times as much wealth as Black graduates with the same degree. In fact, Black Americans with a bachelor's degree hold, on average, a net worth of 72 thousand dollars - eight thousand dollars less wealth than White Americans who never even finish high school and hold an average net worth of 80 thousand dollars. It takes a postgraduate degree for the wealth of Black Americans to compare to that of White Americans who did not finish college. Black Americans with a postgraduate degree average a net worth of about 141 thousand dollars. In comparison, White Americans with "some-college" average about 135 thousand dollars - while White Americans with a postgraduate degree average a net worth of 455 thousand dollars.

A major reason for post-graduate wealth inequality is that, overall, Black college students have to take out a lot more student loans than White students. On average, 41% of college-educated White students receive a college inheritance of over ten thousand dollars, compared to only about 13% of Black Americans. For many students, financial security is the determining factor for completing college, or not. Having an inheritance can have a big impact on the amount of debt incurred.

Furthermore, once college graduates enter the workplace, Black employees earn significantly less than their White counterparts - which impacts the rate they are able to pay back student loans. A 2016 study by the US Department of Education concluded that almost 69% of White bachelor's degree recipients carry about 30 thousand dollars of student loan debt - which they pay back at a rate of 10% per year. In comparison, 85% of Black bachelor's degree recipients carry about 34 thousand dollars of student loan debt - which they pay back at a rate of 4% per year. And that only accounts for graduates who are able to secure employment.

Unequally Employed

Throughout history, African Americans have been accustomed to being the last hired and first fired. Not much has changed over time. Experiencing unemployment restricts anyone's ability to generate wealth. And yet, African Americans are faced with unemployment more often and for longer periods of time. Since their research began in 1972, the US Bureau of Labor Statistics reports that the Unemployment rate for African Americans is almost always double that of White Americans. And while some attribute education and experience as contributing factors to the racial unemployment gap, the fact is, the Unemployment rate is higher for Black people at every education level.

Anytime the entire economy experiences a downfall, unemployment always spikes much higher for African Americans than White Americans. For example, at the peak of The Great Recession - in the years between 2007 and 2009 - Black Americans experienced unemployment at an average rate of 8.2% compared to 3.2% for White Americans. In fact, the median net worth of Black households fell 44% in the years between 2007 and 2013, compared to just 27% for White households. This suggests that the effects of unemployment had a lingering impact on the nation that was significantly harder to bounce back from for Black families.

The recent Movement for Black Lives has drawn new attention to the US's racial wealth and unemployment divide. Unfortunately, this awareness is happening amidst a global health crisis and one of the greatest economic depressions recorded in US history. When the country began to shut down due to the spread of Covid-19 in the spring of 2020, the service industry was hit the hardest. Because people of color are disproportionately employed in service positions, the initial shutdowns left over half of Black Americans unemployed. Nationwide, the Unemployment rate went from 3.5% before the pandemic, and peaked at 14.7% during the pandemic. Overall, the rate of job loss had a similar effect on Black and White Americans. Still, the rate at which people regained employment varied dramatically. By August 2020, over half of White Americans received their jobs back, while just over a third of Black Americans did.

Unequally Paid
On a basic level, income inequality is a major contributing factor in the United States' racial wealth gap. the US experienced economic instability in the first two decades of the 2000s, and the median income fell significantly nationwide. But while the median income for White households rose to 76 thousand dollars by 2019, the median income for Black households only reached 45 thousand dollars. When you dig a little deeper, you will learn that not only are Black people being paid less overall, the majority of jobs held by Black people are less likely to include health insurance, retirement packages, and include less available sick days.

Data from the IASP study found that wage increases are another significant factor in accumulating wealth. During their 25 year study, for every one dollar of increased income, the average White household increased their wealth by $5.19. In the same 25 years, the average Black household only increased by $.69. And for Black households with similar wealth portfolios as White households, their wealth increased by $4.03.

Stunted Growth: Exploring the Racial Wealth Gap

Even when Black people are able to receive income in the top percentile and begin accumulating wealth at some point in their life, they are much more likely than their White counterparts to drop out of that percentile in later years. This is true even for married Black people. During the 25 year study, getting married increased the wealth holdings of White families by 75 thousand dollars, but wealth holdings remained stagnant for Black families or had no significant increase. One reason for this is when high-earning Black families lack pre-existing wealth, they are more likely to have to dip into savings and sell off assets to stay afloat when facing a period of economic instability. Another reason is that high-income Black families are more likely needed to assist lower-income family members. Consequently, very few Black families can sustain emergency savings, have less money to invest, and fewer assets to pass down to future generations.

In general, at every education level, African Americans have always faced challenges with employment throughout US history. Because of this, there has always been a strong presence of entrepreneurship in African American communities. When the economy crashed in 2007, Black Americans experienced an unemployment rate of 8.2% and a 44% decrease in median net worth by 2013. Yet during this time, the amount of black-owned businesses rose 34% by 2012, and 79% by 2017. 95% of these businesses reported having no employees. And about half of these businesses operated in health care, social assistance, repair, maintenance, and other personal services. This suggests that many Black individuals took up entrepreneurship as a means to recoup lost wages.

Nevertheless, the lack of growth for Black-owned businesses has been linked to a lack of funding for them to pay staff, to expand business efforts, and to reserve emergency funding. According to the US Federal Reserve, more than half of Black applicants applying for business loans get rejected. And of the Black applicants that do get approved, only 10% of applicants get fully funded. A lack of emergency funds has left Black businesses particularly vulnerable in the nation's most recent economic downturn. During the months of February to April 2020, the number of Black-owned businesses declined by 41%. In contrast, the number of White-owned businesses declined by merely 17%. Moreover, the Small Business Association reported that by June of 2020, of all the businesses that listed their race only 1.9% of Black companies received federal government relief via the Paycheck Protection Program - compared to 83% of White companies. Unfortunately, being denied access to funding has been a consistent element in the inability to build and sustain wealth in the Black community.

Unequal Land and Homeownership

The most notable explanation for the racial wealth gap in the United States is that only 44% of Black households own their home, compared to 73% of White households. Homeownership is the largest source of wealth for Black families, accounting for 53% of their wealth - compared to 39% of wealth for White families. A recent survey conducted by the home listing website, Zillow, revealed that 59% of Black homebuyers are worried about getting approved for a home loan, compared to 26% of White buyers. This is understandable since Black homebuyers have been denied home loans throughout history at a much higher rate than White people. Even as recent as 2020, a data report by the Home Mortgage Disclosure Act found that lenders deny mortgages for Black applicants at a rate of 80% higher than White applicants.

Black folk have a long history of being denied. After the Civil War, General William T. Sherman issued Special Field Order No. 15. This order confiscated 400 thousand acres of Confederate land along the Atlantic coast of Florida, Georgia, and South Carolina - then divided it among formerly enslaved families. Each household was granted 40 acres and a mule leftover from the war - coining the expression "Forty Acres and A Mule." However, this redistribution of land did not last very long. By May 1865, President Johnson pardoned Confederate soldiers and told them they could have their land back. After that, most Black people had very few other options but to return to their previous plantations and work as sharecroppers - where they were denied ownership of any land.

When Black people finally escaped the South during The Great Migration, they began making significantly more money. Unfortunately, there were virtually no opportunities for them to finance homes. Even when Black families were able to afford the full payment, they were limited to homeownership in all-Black neighborhoods. When attempting to purchase homes in White neighborhoods - which included better schools, less crime, and greater rates of home appreciation - Black homebuyers were met with extreme prejudice from White homeowners who feared their presence would lower the value of their homes. Because of this - and just plain racism - many homeowners, developers, and real-estate agents were required to sign racial covenant contracts preventing them from selling to Black families. Although the Supreme Court ruled that racial covenants were unenforceable in 1948, redlining continued to thrive in cities across the country.

Redlining is when the Home Owners' Loan Corporation, a government-sponsored agency, drew lines around city maps indicating the risk level for long-term real-estate investment - and colored them in red. Race was a blatant factor in determining a "high-risk" area, as Black residents were the common thread among all redlined areas. Initially, these red and green-lined maps were referenced by banks and mortgage lenders to maintain segregation for White homeowners. Yet, eventually, they spread through the entire real estate industry. Banks would find any reason to deny people of color financing for homes outside of red lines. Real-estate contractors used the maps as guides for where they could increase profit margins by overpricing properties and selling them to desperate Black homebuyers. In 1968, The Fair Housing Act legally put an end to redlining, but we can still see its lasting impact on Black wealth. Today, Black homeowners are five times more likely to own a home in a formerly redlined area. When their property value rises, these homeowners increase their wealth by 52% less than homes in formally green-lined areas. Additionally, when the homeownership process is obstructed or blocked entirely, Black Americans are unable to pass down financial education about homeownership to future generations.

Unequal Inheritances and Family Support
The lack of financial support and financial education is another significant factor in racial wealth disparities. Since White families have been building wealth over many generations, they are far more likely to give inheritances. These inheritances can help their children in the form of a downpayment for a home, payment for college tuition, and financial education about building credit and qualifying for loans. In the 25 year IASP study, 36% of White families received an inheritance compared to 7% of Black families. Of the families that received an inheritance, White families received about ten times as much wealth from an inheritance than Black families.

Not only are inheritances contributing less wealth to Black households, but for many long-time homeowners, especially in the South, property inheritances are incredibly vulnerable. Research compounded by ProPublica and The New Yorker found that approximately one-third of all black-owned land in the South is "heirs property." Throughout history, one of the main reasons Black families lose inherited land is because of challenges with proving ownership. For example, many families in rural areas pass on without leaving a will. Their children inherit the property - according to probate laws - then pass it on to their children, and so forth. When land developers and major agricultural corporations seek to acquire their land, the family has been there for generations but is hard-pressed to prove ownership. Without a will, property deed, or some type of binding declaration of ownership, these families do not stand a chance against big-time developers and their lawyers in court. If the family is lucky, developers will offer compensation for their land. Still, the family loses a significant amount of wealth with their loss of ownership. Stories like these are part of the reason Black-owned farmland in the United States plummeted from an estimated 16 million acres in 1910 to three million acres in 2012.

In 2005, the nation witnessed the vulnerability of home-heirs in urban areas when the levees broke and Hurricane Katrina hit the Lower 9th Ward of New Orleans. 70% of houses in that community were damaged, and over one million residents were displaced. When homeowners returned to start rebuilding, 15% of all applicants who applied for federal grants were denied or delayed due to having an "unclear title." For many homeowners, the name on the title was that of a deceased parent or relative. To receive a payout, they had to complete complex procedures to formalize their ownership rights and obtain the signed consent of all eligible heirs. The difficulty of these procedures led to approximately 20 thousand homes left vacant to deteriorate.

Despite all odds, African American homeownership peaked at 46% by the year 2007. Unfortunately, that was the year the US economy crashed and The Great Recession began. Between 2007 and 2016, Black homeowners foreclosed on their homes at a rate of 5%, compared to just 1% for White homeowners. Part of the reason so many Black households foreclosed was that Black homeowners were disproportionately receiving subprime loans in the few years before the recession. After analyzing four million loan applications nationwide, sociologist Jacob William Faber found that Black homeowners were twice as likely to receive subprime loans than White homeowners. In fact, in 2006, Black families earning more than 200 thousand dollars a year were more likely to receive a subprime loan than White families making only 30 thousand dollars a year. Although homeownership increased to 45% by January of 2020, the economic crash due to Covid-19 left more than half of all Black adults unemployed by April. Additionally, by May of 2020, 28% of Black homeowners were deferring their mortgage payment, compared to only 9% of White homeowners. The government could be doing more to assist Black homeowners and enforce fair lending practices, but gerrymandering and voter disenfranchisement make it hard for Black voters to affect change.

Disenfranchised
Political parties in the United States have a long legacy of manipulating Black voters for their own gain. When parties can benefit from the boost in votes, they make it a point to campaign to Black voters. Conversely, when Black voters can potentially harm their agenda, political parties have been known to directly, and indirectly, disenfranchise Black voters. Even when Black people were still enslaved, Southern Democratic slave owners fought to have their slaves recognized in the population so they would receive more seats in Congress and increase their overall political power. In 1787, Congress passed the Three-Fifths Compromise allowing three-fifths of a state's slave population to count toward their total population.

Stunted Growth: Exploring the Racial Wealth Gap

Once emancipated in 1865, 90% of the US Black population lived in the South, and by 1870 the 15th Amendment was passed prohibiting the federal government or any state from denying a person the right to vote based on race or previous servitude. Immediately, Black people attempted to register to vote in large numbers. To extinguish the political contribution Black voters would make to the "anti-slavery" Republican Party, the Democratic Party fought to limit the federal government's power - and began leading efforts to directly disenfranchise the Black vote. These efforts included unjustly incarcerating Black people; enforcing poll taxes; implementing literacy test; requiring frequent re-registration; conducting registration at inconvenient times during planting seasons, then not relaying the time to Black communities; determining an election during a primary, in which Black people were not allowed to participate; as well as physical violence against Black people attempting to register. Even when qualified Black voters were able to navigate all of these deterrents, arbitrary reasons were created to disqualify them from registering. In 1902, James Giles, an eligible Black voter in Mississippi, filed suit against the state on behalf of himself and 75 thousand other qualified Black people who were wrongly denied the right to register. In 1903, The Supreme Court rejected their claim, ruling that if the state was indeed violating the 15th Amendment, then the state was void. Therefore, they could not legally register to vote in a void state.

Though the Republican Party advocated for the abolition of slavery, after emancipation, they intentionally made very little effort to pursue civil rights for African Americans - so that they could garner the support of White Southerners. In the election of 1929, Republican Herber Hoover won the nation's popular and electoral vote by a landslide. Hoover received over two-thirds of the Black vote in this election, even though he integrated himself with segregationists in the South - mainly because Black voters were loyal to the Republican Party and could not fathom aligning themself with the political party that fought to keep them enslaved. During his presidency, the economy was in a dramatic downfall, and the Great Depression left many African Americans unemployed. And while the Republican Party aligned itself more with the racist elite in the South for being pro-business, the Democratic Party began advocating for the government to regulate big businesses and improve the quality of life for all Americans. Because of this, by the 1930s, African Americans increasingly began aligning themselves with the Democratic Party, and White racist Southerners began aligning themselves with the Republican Party. Then in 1965, Democratic President Lyndon B Johnson signed the Voting Rights Act prohibiting racial discrimination in voting. From then on, the majority of African Americans joined the Democratic Party, and the majority of White Southerners joined the Republican Party - and disenfranchising the Black vote became more of a Republican benefit. Even as recent as the 2000s, throughout the nation, we see the Republican Party strategically redrawing district lines - also known as "Gerrymandering" - through and around Black Democratic neighborhoods to extinguish the impact of their vote.

Considering Black Americans have never had a fair shot at the American Dream, they have proven time again that they are more than capable of building wealth and excelling at American democratic capitalism. Still, America continues to stack the cards against them. When Black voters are muted, Black citizens lose the opportunity to influence the laws which govern them. In order to achieve equality, each Black vote needs to be taken into account so that Black people can vote for policies that will have the most significant impact on them. Policies that would reinstate the right to vote for formerly incarcerated individuals. Policies that would decrease the amount of debt plaguing Black college graduates. Policies that could effectively eliminate job discrimination and unequal pay. And policies that could help close the wealth gap through enforcing fair lending practices.

Currently, public policies that are intended to help all Americans rarely trickle down to African Americans. For America to truly be the land of equal opportunity, action needs to be taken at every level to close the racial wealth gap, while taking into account the continued stunted growth of African Americans that structural racism and discrimination are causing.

Stunted Growth: Exploring the Racial Wealth Gap

Eight

A Path Forward

Though the quality of life has undoubtedly improved over time for Black Americans, a long list of racial inequities continues to grow. This list of injustices is increasing because there has never been an effective remedy and repair for enslaving Black people over 150 years ago. The more time that passes without remedy, the more challenging it becomes for younger generations to understand how the unique difficulties Black Americans experience in modern-day society are deeply rooted in the very institution they wish to excel in. Successes of The Civil Rights Movement have given some Black Americans the opportunity to integrate into almost every part of society. And advances in technology provide access to unlimited information with the ability to network with people of all races all over the country. Because of this, the illusion of mobility is often confused with equality. But the fact is, there is hardly a path that young Black Americans can take where they will not encounter racial discrimination. Even though many African Americans do not identify with the term "victim," they are not exempt from experiencing the lingering consequences of unrepaired structural damage. Since effective action was not taken immediately after slavery - to promote nationwide racial healing and provide former slaves with land and the ability to integrate into society - the United States was able to sustain an economy and society in favor of people with white skin. There were many opportunities - post-abolition and before the Jim Crow era - for Congress to set a nationwide precedent for racial equality. Instead, they chose to reinforce institutionalized White supremacy. As a result, the race-based inequities that persist today are not exclusive to the descendants of slaves - they affect all Black people in America at every class level. Likewise, all White people in America benefit from a system of White privilege, whether their ancestors owned slaves or not.

Nevertheless, the future remains optimistic. The more time that passes, it is inevitable that future generations will dismiss skin color to accept and embrace cultural diversity as America's most valuable asset. Once the United States honors its commitment to protect human rights and provide reparations for the damage that institutionalized racism is causing, future generations of Americans will finally benefit from the advantage of having all its citizens equally contributing to society.

Reviewing Our Commitments to Protect Human Rights
The United States adopted the Universal Declaration of Human Rights in order to promote social progress, better standards of living, and an overall better world for everyone. It was also affirmed that everyone has the right to effective remedies and reparations for acts violating these fundamental human rights.

Still, the United States has violated the human rights of its African American citizens in many ways. It forcibly relocated, enslaved, and directly profited from the labor of Black people for almost 250 years. Instead of seeking racial healing after emancipation, the US legalized segregation - authorizing institutional discrimination. Racist acts of violence went unpunished. And the healthcare industry was permitted to use Black people for fatal medical research without consent. To this day, law enforcement in the United States specifically targets Black communities, disproportionately imprisons them, and profits from incarceration. All the while, systematic discrimination against Black Americans inhibits their ability to build generational wealth. Without a doubt, the United States has a moral obligation to provide African Americans remedy and repair for these violations.

Approaching Reparations
Slavery and its legacy is causing integral harm to the United States, on both an institutional and societal level. Providing remedy and repair will require action by both the government and morally responsible individuals and institutions. Federal, state, and local governments can pass into law remedies and reparations that will enforce access to the constitutional rights of Black Americans. They can implement the transformation of institutions rooted in racism and allocate funds for providing compensation and rehabilitation. Meanwhile, individuals, businesses, and private institutions can take moral accountability for perpetuating and benefiting from slavery and systematic racism - then take action towards transforming their own communities.

According to the United Nations Basic Principles and Guidelines on the Right to a Remedy and Reparation, remedies and reparations should include: restitution, compensation, rehabilitation, satisfaction, and a guarantee that it will not happen again. For the remainder of this chapter, we will explore ideas for remedies and reparations using these basic principles as a guide. The following ideas are meant to provoke thoughtful conversation, be considered for adoption, and/or be adapted appropriately. Allow them to inspire you and begin taking action immediately. Let's go!

Restitution

According to the United Nations Basic Principles and Guidelines on the Right to a Remedy and Reparation, restitution should restore victims to their original situation before the gross violations occurred and, as appropriate, include: the restoration of liberty; enjoyment of human rights; restoration of their identity, family life, and citizenship; returning them to their place of residence; restoration of employment; and return of property.

Enslaved Africans were transferred across an entire ocean, so complete restoration as defined above is not possible for their descendants. In this case, solutions will need to adapt to restore the dignity of African Americans on an economic, political, and societal level. How can we restore promises for land given and taken away? How can we restore the rights of Black Americans who were unjustly sent to prison, given unfair and harsh punishments, and tried by racially biased juries? How can we restore the liberty of those who remain in jail because of the inability to pay excessive bail? How can we help African Americans discover their cultural roots and learn their ancestors' origins and history? How can we make up for lost employment opportunities?

Distribution and Redistribution of Land
In the aftermath of the Civil War, General William T. Sherman met with Black community leaders, led by Reverend Garrison Frazier, to gain insight into the needs of newly freed slaves. According to his memoir, General Sherman told Reverend Fraizer, "State in what manner you would rather live, whether scattered among the Whites, or in colonies by yourselves." Reverend Fraizer replied, "by ourselves, for there is a prejudice against us in the South that will take years to get over." Another community leader added, "essentially, we want to be free from the domination of White men, we want to be educated, and we want to own land." Four days later, General Sherman signed Field Order No. 15, which granted thousands of newly freed Black families 40 acres and a mule. Not all freed slaves received land, but for those who did, about ten years later, White Confederates

returned and violently took it all away with permission from President Johnson. Ultimately, Field Order No. 15 was a fail.

Then, in 1866 the Southern Homestead Act was passed to help encourage westward expansion. The act allowed citizens, immigrants, and free Black men to acquire 160 acres of land and improve it for five years to gain ownership. More than 270 million acres of land were granted through this program. Of the approximately 65 hundred claims to land submitted by Black men, most of them were denied. Of those who were given land, only about one thousand of them were granted property certificates. Thus, of the almost four million slaves freed, only one thousand of them were granted land. And of the total 270 million acres of land granted through this act, no more than 160 thousand acres were given to African Americans. The Southern Homestead Act was ultimately another fail for African Americans - but a significant win, and jump-start to wealth building, for White farmers and their families.

Those failed attempts of land distribution were not the only instances where access to land was denied and stripped away from Black people. There have been innumerable times when Black homes, businesses, and entire neighborhoods were burned to the ground by racist mobs of White people. Black-owned farms were unfairly seized by banks and corporations. Black people were legally denied access to homes and communities through racial covenants and red-lining. And although red-lining is now illegal, many Black homebuyers continue to experience racial discrimination in real-estate. White real-estate agents oftentimes avoid showing homes in predominantly White neighborhoods, even when the property is within their Black client's budget. When applying for a home loan, many Black families receive much higher interest rates than their White counterparts at every income level. Since African American's ancestors were transferred across an entire ocean to the United States - and have no land to return to - an appropriate act of restoration for their descendants would be to honor original requests for land - separate from the prejudices and domination of White people.

A Black American couple, Willa and Charles Bruce, migrated west during the Great Migration and purchased ocean-front land in Southern California, in the year 1912. Today, the land rests surrounded by multi-million dollar homes in what is now known as Manhattan Beach. But back then, the beach was affectionately known as "Bruce's Beach." It was one of the few beaches in Southern California where Black people could come and enjoy themselves. Bruce's Beach was an entire resort with a lodge, cafe, nightclub, and other amenities. It grew to be a very popular attraction, and other affluent Black families began purchasing homes nearby. Eventually, White people in the surrounding neighborhoods began terrorizing the community to get them to leave. There are reports of Black people getting their tires slashed, and the KKK lit several homes on fire, including the

Bruce's house. Despite ongoing harassment, this Black community remained steadfast, until the city finally seized the land. In 1924, about 24 Black homeowners were evicted under eminent domain. The city claimed that the area needed a public park right away. There was no park built. The new "public" beach was leased for $1 per year to a White man who only allowed White people access. Along with a few others, the Bruce family sued the city and received a mere 14 thousand dollars in a settlement. The Bruce's were not able to move their resort anywhere else and ended up working as chefs for the rest of their lives. This remains a very painful history for the Bruce family - many of whom have struggled with financial stability. This injustice was all but forgotten until 2007, when the city of Manhattan Beach acknowledged the wrongdoing and decided to rename the area "Bruce's Beach." Then, after years of grassroots lobbying by the family and local community members, Los Angeles County officials voted to return the land back to the family. In addition to land restoration, the family is requesting restitution for the years of lost business and, according to Bruce family descendant, Duane Shepard, "punitive damages for the Manhattan Beach City Council and Police Department for colluding in the plan to terrorize my family and then railroad them out."

Giving the land back to the Bruce descendants and compensating them for lost wages is an excellent example of how local communities and governments can take moral accountability for harm caused, then take action to provide remedy and repair.

Additionally, the US government can offer individuals and institutions an incentive to vacate former slave-holding farms, plantations, homes, buildings, and former confederate land along the east coast, and give it to African Americans.

To increase homeownership and narrow the racial wealth gap, the US government can work with banks to waive property taxes and offer no-interest home loans to African Americans.

Groups of morally responsible White people can pool their money to help pay off the mortgage for their African American neighbors. And the federal government can provide incentives by allowing these contributions to be deducted from their taxes.

Local governments can grant vacant homes in their district to African American residents, and offer a stipend for repairs.

How else do you think the US government could redistribute and grant land to the African American descendants of slaves?

In what ways do you think morally responsible individuals, businesses, and institutions can take part in redistribution efforts?

How do you think the US government and communities can work together to provide restitution by way of land ownership to the living descendants of slaves?

Restoration of Rights for The Incarcerated
The Bill of Rights states that no US citizen should be deprived of life, liberty, or property without due process. It says that in all criminal prosecutions, the accused shall enjoy the right to a speedy and public trial by an impartial jury of the state and district. They should have the assistance of counsel for their defense and be confronted with the witnesses against them - and there should be a compulsory process for obtaining witnesses in their favor. It also states that excessive bail should not be required, excessive fines should not be imposed, nor cruel and unusual punishments inflicted. Unfortunately, Black citizens of the US do not have full and fair access to these rights.

Historically, African Americans have been targeted to fill prison cells - taking away their freedom and right to vote. Even for the hundreds of thousands of eligible voters in jail awaiting trial, many of them lack access to information about dates, deadlines, absentee ballots, and other essential information. In all but three states, prison reform efforts have succeeded in restoring the right to vote for formerly incarcerated people. Still, in some states, voter eligibility is determined by which type of crime you were convicted of. And in others, requirements such as "proof of release" make it nearly impossible to register. Additionally, being incarcerated significantly reduces employment opportunities. Not being able to work decreases the ability to relocate from a community targeted by police and increases the chance of being incarcerated again.

When someone is incarcerated for any amount of time, their family is disadvantaged by the financial burden of having to come up with the money for associated fees. They also have one less contributing member in the household and one less parent and/or childcare provider. Moreover, targeting and criminalizing Black people perpetuates negative stereotypes that keep police and society afraid of Black people - creating a revolving cause and effect. Which came first, the chicken or the egg? In this case, we know the answer. Targeting Black people to fill prisons with unjust laws came before mass incarceration and the intentional creation of a criminal class of Black people. It is the reason why, to this day, Black people disproportionately fill prisons in every US state and territory. So, how can we restore the rights of currently and formerly incarcerated Black people? Here are a few ideas...

Reparations Handbook

The US government, law firms, and elected juries can work together to grant a retrial, with quality representation, to everyone in prison with a plea deal. It should be required that juries include the accused person's local community members and racial and economic-adjacent peers. Everyone who is proven innocent should be immediately released, compensated for their time served, and have all their rights restored.

Additionally, courts, lawyers, and bail bondsmen can refund all fees incurred to everyone found innocent of a crime they were convicted of. Moving forward, there should be strict guidelines and substantial evidence and/or witness testimonies required before someone is eligible for a plea deal.

Congress should pass a federal law that recognizes all facilities holding people awaiting trial as polling stations. Everyone not yet found guilty should be provided a valid voting ballot, and staff should ensure these votes are accurately counted in the election.

Everyone in prison serving a mandatory minimum sentence for a non-violent offense should be granted "time-served" and be immediately released.

Everyone in prison for marijuana-related crimes should be immediately released in states where marijuana is now legal. The same for any other drug or criminal offense. They should also receive compensation for years spent in jail after the legalization went into effect.

N'COBRA proposes that all African American political prisoners should be pardoned and immediately released.

Congress can enact a federal law to automatically restore the right to vote for anyone formerly incarcerated. They can also prohibit state and local governments from adding additional requirements for their voter registration.

Employers can remove all questions about criminal history from their employment applications. Or perhaps only require applicants to provide a brief explanation if they were convicted of a specified crime related to the job. For example, a retail position would require a brief explanation if convicted of theft. And applicants should be allowed to explain the circumstances of their conviction, how long ago the crime happened, or if they were wrongly convicted.

In what ways do you think governments, businesses, and institutions can provide remedy and restoration for Black people who are unfairly incarcerated or formerly incarcerated?

What are some ways you and your community can help restore formerly incarcerated people's rights and dignity?

Currently, inmates with cell phones are sharing clips of their everyday life. In their videos they post what they eat, their daily routine, and how they generally feel. As a result, their videos are going viral - people are beginning to identify with the prisoners and find common ground. For many, watching these videos has inspired an unexpected sense of compassion and empathy.

What other ways can we as a society eliminate the negative stigma of those who were formerly incarcerated?

Ancestry Insight
When Africans were transferred to the United States, they were separated from their families and taken to an unknown land. They were forbidden to speak their native language and prevented from reading and writing. Many cultural practices were forbidden, and a White-led religion and lifestyle were forced upon them. When slavery ended, the US doubled down on White supremacy. And despite many advances in civil rights, society continues to incentivize Black people for assimilating to whiteness. Consequently, the cultural practices, languages, history, and origins of African American's ancestors have been lost.

The vast majority of African Americans do not know the country their ancestors were transferred from or anything about their cultural roots. Providing access to ancestry insight is an essential form of reparations that would help restore dignity and provide historical context for their current whereabouts. It could offer insight into inherited behaviors and best health practices intended for someone with their particular genetic makeup. The US government and morally responsible genealogy companies can work together to help African Americans discover their ancestral roots. Ancestry.com has extensive census and other historical records that help reveal ancestry information. They also provide a guide, specifically for African Americans, for how to use their data to uncover information about enslaved relatives. Through Ancestory.com, many African Americans have learned which plantation their ancestors were enslaved on and even the exact ship they were brought over. Companies like 23andMe help many African Americans discover their ancestral regions and migration history. Additionally, they provide health records that include: genetic diseases you may be susceptible to and carrier traits you may have.

Helping to restore identity and family life through ancestry insight is so important. It can be an incredibly impactful remedy and provide medical and cultural understanding to a race of Americans who were robbed of their family history.

The US government can undoubtedly sponsor genetic testing for everyone who identifies as African American as a form of reparations.

What other ideas do you think could help descendants of enslaved Africans restore their identity and family life?

Affirmative Action and Inclusion Programs
Historically, inalienable rights granted to citizens in the United States were intended and reserved for people with white skin. These rights included citizenship, the right to vote, land and homeownership, employment, education, freedom of speech, the right to carry a gun, and many others. Over time, laws were enacted to extend these rights to African Americans. Yet, racial discrimination continues to result in unequal access to education and employment opportunities - both of which are significant contributors to wealth building and upward social mobility.

To ease some of the racial tension being caused by ongoing discrimination, affirmative action programs were enacted in the late 1960s by President Lyndon B Johnson. In a commencement speech at Howard University in 1965, President Johnson acknowledged unfair inequities in socioeconomic advancements for African Americans due to the lack of remedy and reparations after slavery. He affirmed, "You do not take a person who for years has been hobbled by chains... liberate him, bring him up to the starting line of a race, and then say 'You are free to compete with all the others - and still justly believe that you have been completely fair." The Johnson administration's affirmative action programs were designed and enforced to actively include African Americans and other minority groups in schools and workplaces where they have been traditionally underrepresented or excluded because of their race. These policy programs require that all federally funded institutions diversify their establishments through outreach campaigns and provide people of color with support groups. Additionally, the government provided federal funding and government contracts to private institutions that chose to adopt affirmative action programs while reserving the right to deny them if they practiced discrimination.

Almost immediately, these policies received backlash and pushback. Since employers and universities only have space to admit a specific number of applicants, White people who would otherwise be filling those positions argue that affirmative action is essentially reverse racism. Although the intention was to only admit qualified applicants in work and educational spaces, affirmative action opponents say that institutions are lowering the standard of eligibility for African Americans and solely accepting them based on race - which contributes to the stereotypes that Black people are less intelligent and less capable. Many cases have been brought to the Supreme Court, suing institutions on the basis that admitting applicants based on race is reverse discrimination and an ineffective way to fight against inequality. Ultimately, the Supreme Court decided to uphold affirmative action policies as long as institutions did not use racial quotas in the admittance process.

Although affirmative action practices remain highly controversial, the fact is, they have proven to be effective in providing many Black Americans educational and employment opportunities they were previously excluded from. According to the National Center for Educational Statistics, the impact of these policies resulted in a 10 to 13% increase in college enrollment of Black Americans between 1976 and 2008. A report by Fidan Ana Kurtulus at the Upjohn Institute for Employment Research found that as a direct result of affirmative action policies, Black Americans received a substantial increase in federal contract jobs between the years 1973 and 2003. Becoming a federal contractor increased employment shares by 87% for Black women and between 60% to 396% for Black men. Additionally, the study found employers continued to hire African Americans and other minority groups well after their affirmative action program ended. This suggests that affirmative action policies contributed significantly to long-term diversity in workplaces.

The Unrelenting opposition to affirmative action policies indicates that eventually, they will fade away. Meanwhile, the recent outpouring of support for racial justice suggests that these policies could be replaced by other forms of inclusion programs. In the years between 1996 and 2020, ten states banned affirmative action policies altogether. But also, in 2020, the United States experienced an unprecedented racially diverse uprising against overt and institutionalized racism against Black Americans. Businesses and institutions perpetuating racism were boycotted, while White people who were caught on camera weaponizing their White privilege were publicly humiliated, and many lost their jobs. As such, many companies began to align themselves with the Black Lives Matter movement - publicly declaring their support and taking immediate action towards implementing racial-sensitivity workshops and diversity training. Fortune 500 companies, mom-and-pop shops, and every size company in between made public commitments to increase Black leadership in their companies.

In the year 2020, morally responsible citizens of all races used social media outlets to express their disapproval, publicly shame, and organize massive boycotts of companies found perpetuating racism. This large-scale act of grassroots activism compelled many companies to create their own diversity inclusion strategies similar to, and in some cases more aggressive than, the affirmative action policies implemented by the Johnson administration. For example, Delta Airlines committed to doubling the number of Black people in leadership roles from 7% to

14% by the year 2025. Estee Lauder committed to increasing Black representation over the next five years by hiring one Black person for every seven to eight hirees at every level in the company. Expressing verbal and financial support for companies championing racial justice - while expressing public disapproval and boycotting companies committing racial injustices - has proven to be an effective way of restoring employment opportunities for Black Americans.

What other ways do you think morally responsible individuals and communities can work together to hold employers accountable for ending systematic and cultural racism in the workplace?

How do you think the US government can help support diversity inclusion and ensure diverse leadership in the workplace?

How can morally responsible citizens apply pressure and compel universities to lean into diversity inclusion?

Furthermore, how can affirmative action policies be improved to provide more comprehensive and socially accepted methods of admitting African American applicants, while providing support to African American students as an intentional form of reparations?

Compensation and Rehabilitation

According to the United Nations Basic Principles and Guidelines on the Right to a Remedy and Reparation, compensation should be provided for any economic damage the violation caused, such as physical or mental harm; lost opportunities for employment, education or social benefits; moral damage; and compensation for any costs required for legal or expert assistance, medicine, medical services, psychological services, and social services.

Rehabilitation should include medical and psychological care, as well as legal and social services.

Providing compensation and rehabilitation to African Americans is a necessary form of reparations that can help shrink the racial wealth gap in America. African Americans have proven the ability to excel in American democratic capitalism. Still, ongoing racial discrimination and opportunity-inequality obstruct the overall ability to build and sustain wealth for many. Compensation and rehabilitation can also provide healthcare for the mental, emotional, and intergenerational injuries sustained by racial trauma. Furthermore, it is deeply traumatic to be disconnected from your ancestral roots and to exist in a country that perpetuates a racial hierarchy and institutionalizes race-based discrimination - all while minimizing and devaluing the pain inflicted by doing so.

So how can the US provide compensation for the generational wealth amassed on the backs of Black slaves yet denied to their descendants? How can we ensure that descendants of the very slaves that built America's elite educational institutions will have an opportunity to obtain an elite education? How can we ensure that Black people will have access to quality legal representation when being tried in America's racially biased justice system? And in what ways can we ensure that Black Americans will be provided with quality, comprehensive health and psychiatric care?

Cash Payments
Despite extensive data on race-based wealth inequality in the United States, reparations in the form of cash payments remains highly controversial.

Immediately after abolishing slavery, there was virtually no economic support or access to work opportunities for African Americans. Furthermore, discrimination in the workplace and institutional racism has led to ongoing employment inequalities and wage gaps. Because of this, there has always been a substantial wealth gap. To this day, the median wealth holdings for the average White American is almost ten times the amount of the average Black American. In some cities, the racial wealth gap is even more extreme. For example, in 2015, the Federal Reserve of Boston reported that White households held a median wealth of $247,500, while the median wealth of Black households was only $8. Ongoing studies suggest the racial wealth gap is so wide, it will never close unless substantial payments are made to intentionally supplement decades of lost income for African Americans.

Still, many people - even many advocates for reparations - are opposed to cash payments. Arguments against cash payments include: How can you put a price on the pain and suffering of slavery? Because of racism, it is highly unlikely the US will provide Black Americans reparations in the form of cash - it would be more effective to broaden requests to include other forms of reparations. To simply give cash to Black people is an ineffective way to remedy racial wealth inequality - the majority of the money will be spent enriching White-owned companies. Cash payments to Black Americans would harm the economy. We should focus on closing the wealth gap for all Americans - wealthy Black Americans do not need reparations. Living African Americans were not slaves, so why should they receive payments? Living White Americans never owned slaves, so why should they have to pay? Racism was legal at the time, so there should be no penalty for slavery. the US has committed human rights violations against many groups - why only give money to Black people? Giving money to Black Americans contributes to a victim mentality and promotes dependency - you should "teach a man to fish." And - Giving reparations to Black Americans will further divide Americans.

Some of these arguments are rooted in genuine concern. But many are used to diminish the need for reparations and avoid solving a problem that people in opposition are frankly uninterested in solving. Nevertheless, it is necessary to address concerns about cash payments in a way that focuses on the need for economic justice for African Americans - and to create an equitable society for everyone. The following responses are intended to inspire ideas for answers you can use, transform, or build upon when making a case for reparations in the form of cash payments.

Friendly Reminder:
Keep in mind, it is neither appropriate nor effective for a community benefiting from the oppression of another community to also decide how that oppressed community should be repaired or compensated.

Concern:
How can you put a price on the pain and suffering of slavery?

Response:
There is no possible way to quantify the pain and loss endured during slavery. Still, cash payments are an imperative form of economic justice.

There have been decades of research and thoughtful analysis to calculate the amount of money that should be distributed. Larry Neal, an economist at the University of Illinois, Champaign/Urbana, proposed that the lost wages from slavery between the years 1620 and 1840 would amount to 1.4 trillion dollars. Richard Vedder, an economist at Ohio University, estimated 5 to 10 trillion dollars as an accumulated gain in wealth for White Southerners. Journalist Tim Worstall used the market value of an enslaved person to calculate the total wealth of having slaves as an asset. He then compounded 1% to estimate a total of 1.75 trillion dollars - or about 40 thousand dollars per person - as the amount owed to each African American descendant. In her article, "Restitution for American Slavery: a Forensic Science Approach," economist Sibblye Scholz adds the three most essential components of slavery - lost wages, the value of slaves, and the lost promise of forty acres and a mule - then estimates that an accumulated wealth would amount to 3.83 trillion dollars. These estimates are a valuable contribution to calculating the amount of compensation African Americans should be paid in reparations. But they do not include the inequality of paid wages, lost employment opportunities, the inability to access higher education, and the inability to accumulate assets over time.

Concern:
Because of racism, it is highly unlikely the US will give Black Americans reparations in the form of cash - it would be more effective to broaden requests to include other forms of reparations.

Response:
i acknowledge this argument is often made by advocates with genuine concern who hope to achieve tangible results - people who intend no offense. However, this argument perpetuates the idea that Black people are low-ranking citizens. Eligibility for justice should not be determined by race. Additionally, it is more effective to advocate clearly and directly for the goal we want to achieve.

When the goal was to end segregation, the argument was made in the case of Brown v. Board of Education that separate was inherently unequal. As a result, the Supreme Court ruled that segregation was entirely unconstitutional. Suppose the argument was simply to provide equal schools for Black people in a segregated society. In that case, we may still be living in a Jim Crow era.

The goal of cash payments is to achieve economic justice for African Americans and create an equitable society for all Americans. Accordingly, we must assert the data and research that prove racial wealth divides will persist unless African Americans receive substantial cash payments to remedy decades of lost income. Even when racism ceases to exist in the United States, data proves that the racial gap will continue. The only way to achieve economic justice for African Americans is to distribute cash payments - allowing the fair opportunity to grow their own wealth.

Concern:
To simply give cash to Black people is an ineffective way to remedy racial wealth inequality - the majority of the money will be spent enriching White-owned companies.

Response:
i acknowledge this is also an argument often made with genuine concern. Nevertheless, the way people choose to spend their money is their own business. i suspect there will be many all-Black investment groups that will intentionally build wealth by investing in Black communities, Black-owned companies, and creating Black-owned institutions. i suspect there will be many Black people who choose to

invest their money into real-estate, stocks, retirement, college education, trust funds for their children, and starting new businesses. i suspect that many people will use the money to pay off their debts and have little left over to invest. i also suspect that many people will splurge on fashion, cars, technology, vacations, and extravagant nights at the club. Whatever the case, Black Americans should have the opportunity to choose their fate. The opportunity to choose is empowering and provides economic justice in the most sincere form.

Perhaps the most effective way to prevent the concern of enriching White-owned businesses is to provide as much education as possible and attempt to instill a set of values that prioritize wealth-building in the Black community. If your passion is to increase the success of Black-owned businesses and/or encourage Black entrepreneurship, you will make an excellent person to provide this education. Begin it.

Concern:
Cash payments to Black Americans would harm the economy.

Response:
There is an equal chance that providing large lump sums of money to African Americans would be great for the economy. If those who are given cash payments add to the nation's production of goods and create more jobs, there may be more rewards than drawbacks. Be that as it may, the effect on the economy is hypothetical and unpredictable. In their book, *From Here to Equality*, William A. Darity and A. Kristen Mullen suggest that reparation payments be made over a period of time to avoid inflation and other harmful effects on the economy.

In addition to strategic payouts, providing education on how the economy works and best practices for wealth-building would also help ensure that recipients spend in a way that has an overall positive effect. There are many creative solutions to this problem. Avoiding economic justice because of a lack of imagination should not be an option.

Concern:
We should focus on closing the wealth gap for all Americans - wealthy Black Americans do not need reparations.

Response:
When the topic at hand is how to provide remedy and repair to African Americans for slavery and its legacy of discrimination and income inequality, we must stay focused on that.

Cash payments serve as an intentional form of economic justice for African Americans. By the time slavery ended in 1865, much of the country's wealth and high-class society had already been established. The vast majority of African Americans were thrust into poverty. A smaller portion of African Americans were able to work and finance a new life - those who were free and working before the Civil War, soldiers who earned money from fighting in the war, and even former slaves who could use their skills to earn wages. A very small fraction of African Americans were so successful in business they became millionaires soon after emancipation. In the decades to come, African Americans steadily worked together to build up their own communities, businesses, and economies. All of their success was achieved despite being confronted with ongoing discrimination, destruction of property, theft of savings in the bank, businesses being shut down by targeted attacks using unfair legal practices, the inability to access credit, unequal access to homeownership, the ongoing threat of violence, and much more.

Over time, Black people have been conditioned to persevere under extreme circumstances. Just like every other citizen, African Americans deserve a fair shot at achieving the American dream of upward economic mobility. Withholding payments to wealthy Black Americans, or to suggest they "don't need the money," is essentially suggesting a limit should be placed on the amount of wealth Black people should be allowed to accumulate. In a capitalist country, if White families are allowed to build and sustain extreme amounts of generational wealth with money earned in a slave economy, African American families should have the opportunity to do the same in our modern economy.

However, suppose the nation makes a democratic decision to redistribute wealth or begin awarding citizens a minimum wage. In that case, payments should be distributed to African Americans to intentionally eliminate the racial wealth gap. For example, in their Reparations Toolkit, the Movement for Black Lives proposes a universal basic income for all adults in the United States - with an additional prorated amount distributed over time to African Americans.

Senator Cory Booker proposes another idea for closing the nation's wealth gap through baby bonds - a trust that would compound yearly payments to everyone in the country. The amount would depend on the family's current wealth holdings. Those who make more would receive less, and those who make less would receive more. Over time, this type of supplemental income is projected to close the wealth gap in the US - particularly African American families who disproportionately have lower wealth holdings.

Both are great ideas that can be further developed to achieve economic justice for African Americans and a more equitable economy for everyone.

Concern:
Living African Americans were not slaves, so why should they receive payments?

Response:
Every Black person in the United States experiences the effects of racism upheld by the US government immediately after slavery. There were many occasions for the United States government to encourage nationwide racial healing, provide economic support to African Americans, and enforce racial inclusion. Instead, those opportunities were taken to reinforce racial hierarchies in society. As a result, African American communities have faced ongoing economic inequalities.

Recent data reveals that African Americans experience persistent wealth inequality, gaps in earned income, inequality in job opportunities, more extended periods of unemployment, higher interest loans than White people with the exact same credit and wealth portfolio, unequal access to homeownership in high-income neighborhoods, and much more. Many of these economic inequalities are rooted in the implicit biases perpetuated by racist media. Nevertheless, pathways to wealth building remain obstructed. Black Americans did not have to experience slavery to experience the ongoing effects of racist discrimination and unfair access to wealth building.

Concern:
Living White Americans never owned slaves, so why should they have to pay?

Response:
Every White person in the United States experiences the effects of racism upheld by the US government immediately after slavery. There were many occasions for the United States to encourage nationwide racial healing, provide economic support to African Americans, and enforce racial inclusion. Instead, those opportunities were taken to reassure White Americans that they are superior citizens. Throughout history, White people have been prioritized over Black people in the job market, the judicial system, the housing market, at educational institutions, and for lending and investments. Additionally, they are given the benefit of the doubt more often when it comes to achieving financial success. As a result, White people have been able to streamline paths to financial stability and generational wealth building in ways Black Americans have never been able to.

Data reveals that White families hold almost ten times the amount of wealth as Black families. White people are paid more, given larger raises, and are extended better benefits in the workplace. They are less likely to experience prolonged periods of unemployment. And they are granted access to high-value homes at lower interest rates than Black people with the exact same credit and wealth portfolio. The list goes on.

Many White people recognize these inequities but are unwilling to participate in reparations if it means sacrificing their privilege. Nevertheless, i would like to offer an alternative perspective. To secure the future of your economic and social position, it is best to do whatever you can to usher in a new value system rooted in equal access to economic opportunity. Continuing to support systems rooted in racial hierarchy leaves every race vulnerable to institutional privilege or oppression.

Concern:
Racism was legal at the time, so there should be no penalty for slavery.

Response:
The United States made a moral commitment to protect human rights and provide reparations to those whose human rights they violate. Slavery, segregation, genocide, and mass incarceration are a shortlist of human rights violations committed by and/or sanctioned by the United States against African Americans. There have been several times in US history where the country took accountability for violating the human rights of other minority groups - for whom reparations were given in the form of cash payments. To withhold economic justice to African Americans is a continuation of the race-based discrimination that we ultimately aim to put an end to.

Furthermore, reparations are not a form of punishment or penalty.

Awarding reparations to African Americans is a vital step in achieving economic justice for a group of people who were specifically enslaved to build the nation's foundation of wealth then thrust into poverty when emancipated. A group of people who continue to face oppression because of inaction taken to promote racial healing and implement equal access to wealth-building opportunities.

Equally as important, providing reparations is a way to begin taking action to replace value systems rooted in racism with values rooted in equality.

Concern:
The US has committed human rights violations against many groups - why only give money to Black people?

Response:
Indeed, the US has committed human rights violations against many groups. The US has also provided remedy and repair for many of those groups. Deprioritizing

economic justice for African Americans perpetuates that African Americans are less deserving of the same rights everyone else is entitled to. Suggesting that the well-being of Black citizens is not a priority, naturally minimizes the impact of contributions they made to the country's success.

Additionally, the potential contributions and successes African Americans will achieve when operating on level ground should not be underestimated. Black people have achieved an incredible amount of success in the face of extreme prejudice and violence. Imagine the contributions that African Americans will make to the country when there is an even foundation to build upon.

Concern:
Giving money to Black Americans contributes to a victim mentality and promotes dependency - you should "teach a man to fish."

Response:
This is an offensive statement. Reparations are not a form of welfare, and anyone with a pole can fish.

Throughout history, Black people have been routinely denied equal access to higher education, homeownership, credit, leadership positions in the workplace, networking events, and much more. Amid great adversity, Black people persevere the best they can with what they have. Reparations in the form of cash payments serve as a hand-up, not a handout. They are meant to help remedy the years of denied access to economic mobility - which created the extreme and ongoing racial wealth gaps in the United States.

Concern:
Giving reparations to Black Americans will further divide Americans.

Response:
The goal of reparations - particularly in cash payments - is to intentionally close gaps, not widen them.

This concern is rooted in racism and perpetuates the idea that Americans will continue to operate in racism even when intentional efforts are made to create a more equitable society. To this, i offer an alternative perspective - the increased opportunity to build wealth for one person does not decrease the opportunity to build wealth for another. Americans of all backgrounds can live a dignified life at the same time. The Treasury of the United States has plenty of money to invest. Individual White people have nothing to lose but their pride.

In short, the goal of providing cash payments to African Americans is a necessary form of reparations. Economists estimate that African Americans are owed billions to trillions of dollars in back pay for slavery and confiscated land. Regardless, with an equal opportunity to work, earn, and achieve without adversity, the amount of wealth African Americans could have amassed would be many times more than what it is. Reparations distributed intentionally to empower African Americans to choose their economic future is one of the most effective ways the US can help remedy the damage caused and eliminate the racial wealth gap. When making a case for providing economic justice in the form of cash payments, it is important to remain unwavering.

Free Education and Student Loan Forgiveness
Studies on building wealth have proven that obtaining a college degree significantly increases the amount of wealth a household is able to accumulate - but that amount is much less for Black graduates than White graduates in the US. This is in part because Black students are more likely to graduate with greater amounts of student loan debt. In fact, in 2016, the US Department of Education reported that Black students graduate with more student debt than any other race. Studies show that the giant shadow of student loan debt is a prominent reason students drop out of college. And those who drop out have a more difficult time repaying the debt they collected while there.

Additionally, the Institute on Asset and Social Policy found that Black students accumulate more debt in college because the average Black student enters college with less inheritance in their college fund, leaving them needing to borrow more. Moreover, there is a huge wage gap between Black and White employees post-graduation, which directly impacts the rate at which they are able to repay student loans.

Although more Black students are attending college than ever before, their debt is higher than ever. In 2019, one in four Black Americans between the ages of 25 and 29 held a college degree. Meanwhile, a College Board study on trends in college pricing found that between 1988 and 2018, college tuition rose by 213% - and is expected to continue rising. Furthermore, the amount of federal funding designated to public universities is decreasing, and tuition costs can be more than double at for-profit universities. Julia Barnard, a student debt expert at the Center for Responsible Lending, explains that Black students are disproportionately targeted by for-profit colleges and a larger civil rights issue is at play. More than 25% of Black students attend for-profit colleges compared to only 10% of White students.

Reparations Handbook

According to a study in 2018 by the Samuel Dubois Cook Center for Equity Development and the Insight Center for Community Economic Development, the median net worth for Black graduates is around 70 thousand dollars, but it is about 268 thousand for White graduates. As a matter of fact, the average net worth for Black graduates is still ten thousand dollars less than the average net worth of White Americans who never finish high school. These racial disparities in net worth highlight the Undeniable impact that being historically denied access to higher education - while graduating with large amounts of student loan debt - continues to have on Black graduates and their ability to build and sustain wealth. This is terribly ironic since many educational institutions were funded by selling slaves and the tuition paid by slave labor. So how can we remedy and repair the economic damage that unequal access to affordable higher education has caused African Americans? Here are a few ideas…

Access to education was one of the initial requests by the freedmen who met with General Sherman immediately after the Civil War. As such, awarding African American students free tuition - and offering student loan forgiveness for debts already incurred - would be an appropriate remedy and reparation helping to increase the amount of wealth Black graduates have, and can, accumulate.

Many morally responsible education institutions and their students have studied and taken accountability for their participation in the slave trade - and are now developing plans to provide reparations. For example, Georgetown University has a deeply rooted foundation of wealth directly afforded by slave labor. Profits from slave labor kept tuition free at the University from its establishment in 1789 until 1832. Then, in 1838, 272 slaves were sold by Georgetown University's president, which funded a massive scale-up for their campus. 181 years later, in 2019, two-thirds of Georgetown University students voted in a referendum to increase their tuition by $27.20 each semester (totaling around 380 thousand dollars a year) to create a reparations fund benefiting the descendants of the 272 slaves sold. The University later announced that it planned to take action with the student's decision. Although they will not be implementing the $27.20 raise in tuition, they plan to allocate funds for reparations equal to or greater than the amount student fees would have raised.

While the student's referendum vote to increase tuition is not being implemented, the idea to increase tuition by a small amount to create a large-scale reparations fund is a great idea. If every university which participated in slavery agreed to increase tuition by $20 per semester to create a reparations fund - a fund that would specifically contribute to the tuition of its African American students - millions of dollars could be awarded each year. This would make a profound difference in the lives of those African American students while impacting individual university students very little.

Another impactful and appropriate way to monetarily support access to higher education is to fully fund historically black colleges and universities (HBCUs). HBCUs are a consistent pillar of empowerment in Black communities. They have traditionally provided their students with a supportive learning environment and continue to carry a legacy of success. Although HBCUs cost less than predominantly White colleges, they account for about 27% of all low-income Black college students. As such, HBCU students take out twice as much student loan debt. Still, overall, their graduates are more financially successful than Black graduates of non-HBCUs. In fact, a survey of 60 thousand college and university graduates found that, across the board, graduates of HBCUs report having greater purpose well-being, social well-being, financial well-being, community well-being, and physical well-being than Black graduates of predominantly White schools. Furthermore, 55% of HBCU graduates reported that they believe their university prepared them well for life outside of college - compared to 29% of Black graduates from non-HBCUs. HBCU graduates account for 80% of all Black judges, 50% of Black lawyers, 40% of Black congressmen, 40% of Black engineers, 12.5% of Black CEOs, 50% of Black non-HBCU professors, and 40% of Black undergraduates in STEM programs. Over the years, HBCU enrollment has consistently been on the decline, and so has their federal and state funding. Nevertheless, the environment they provide Black students has proven safer from racial biases and effective in producing prosperous graduates. As long as there are students interested in attending historically Black colleges and universities, they must receive whatever funding needed to continue providing a thriving learning environment for their students.

In addition to public colleges and universities, the Movement of Black Lives introduced a reparations proposal that demands free access to technical education programs - including technology, trade, and agricultural programs.

Morally responsible schools and education programs can award full scholarships to their African American students. The US government can offer tax write-offs and federal funding to incentivize them to do so.

The US government can also offer tax write-offs and other incentives for morally responsible individuals who choose to cover the cost of tuition for Black students.

In what other ways can the US government can ensure that African American students are compensated with free college and university education?

What other ways can morally responsible institutions and communities cover the cost of tuition for African Americans as a form of remedy and reparation?

Free Quality Legal Defenders

Until the entire United States justice system and law enforcement are completely replaced, uprooted from racism, and unaffected by implicit bias, Black Americans must be provided a comprehensive and quality legal defense. Surely, systematic mass incarceration is one of the most horrific consequences of the inaction taken to promote nationwide racial healing and enforce racial equality. When slaves were granted their freedom, they were immediately targeted to fill prisons by racist people legally enacting racist policies. Just five years after emancipation African Americans made up 95% of the southern prison population. Once convicted, they were leased to businesses and forced to work as punishment. Before ever going to trial, many accused were bailed out by businessmen who would offer to pay the court a "surety" for their release in exchange for their labor. Then, when the number of people accused exceeded the capacity of courts to process them, the accused would be intimidated into signing "confess judgments". They were coerced to plead guilty in exchange for an automatic conviction with the promise of having to serve less time without ever going to trial. Incarcerating African Americans in large numbers allowed this system to gain the momentum needed to make a substantial economic impact. This system was so lucrative for states, it burst at the seams with African Americans and expanded to include socially undesirable, low-income Americans of every race.

According to a study by The Prison Policy Initiative, in 2017, the US criminal justice industry was estimated to be over 182 billion dollars. Businessmen who once paid the courts a "surety" for someone's release in exchange for their labor evolved into a multi-billion dollar bail bond industry. Instead of providing bail bondsmen labor for a "surety," they are now required to pay the bail bondsmen a large fee with a lot of interest. The majority of jail inmates cannot afford bail bond services - they remain in jail awaiting trial, generating a profit while there. The immoral agreements once known as "confess judgments" are now infamously known as "plea bargains" or "plea deals." And currently, those who accept those agreements account for over 95% of both state and federal prison inmates.

Although this system of injustice is officially a human rights violation affecting Americans of all races, African Americans continue to be blatantly targeted by law enforcement and disproportionately represented in prisons. At Black Lives Matter rallies - protesting police for murdering Black men - it is common to hear the chant "the whole damn system is guilty as hell." Guilty indeed, of gross human rights violations committed against its own citizens. For African Americans to receive a fair and fighting chance in a system successfully designed to generate wealth by attacking them, they must receive free quality and comprehensive legal representation as a form of reparations.

The US government should compensate morally responsible law offices and individual legal defenders generously enough to ensure defenders can dedicate quality time, research, and resources to each African American client.

Qualified defendants should also be required to complete educational training in the history and nuances of Black criminalization.

In what other ways do you think the US government and morally responsible legal defenders can compensate African Americans with free legal services as a form of remedy and reparation?

Free Mental and Physical Health Care
It is traumatic to experience violence, discrimination, defamation, and belittlement over generations because of your skin color. The trauma worsens when having to prepare your children to survive and operate under in same or similar circumstances. The politics of being Black in the United States carries both blatant and subconscious psychological and physical health stressors. Having to validate yourself as worthy of human rights in a country you helped build, then having to continue to advocate over generations for that country to protect you from the abuse they conditioned the dominant race to commit against you... it is exhausting. The violence and discrimination the United States allows against Black Americans diminishes trust in authority and instills insecurity, paranoia, and other symptoms that parallel those who have experienced traumatic stress. In her book *Post Traumatic Slave Syndrome*, Dr. Joy Degruy describes vacant esteem, ever present anger, and racist socialization as symptoms occurring in a population that experienced multigenerational trauma resulting from centuries of slavery, continued oppression, and institutionalized racism.

Most notably, ever since emancipation, Black people have suffered physical violence at the hands of police, who have been taught to fear and target them as criminals. But perhaps more common is the suffering caused when Black Americans have to shrink, belittle, or humiliate themselves to be accepted by their community. For example, it is not uncommon for Black creators and entrepreneurs to recruit a White person to join their venture to validate their work and appeal to a larger audience. Likewise, quite a few of the wealthiest Black businessmen in American history have shared stories where they called on a White friend or partner to pose as them to close a deal - they would have otherwise lost due to racial discrimination.

Even though modern civil rights laws and diverse representation on the internet can present an illusion of equality in America, in reality, Black Americans have to constantly be aware of how they present themselves in society - as to not be perceived as lower class, or worse, as a threat by the very people who have historically caused them harm. As recent as March 2021, author Amanda Gorman shared her experience with this form of institutionalized gaslighting when she tweeted, "A security guard tailed me on my walk home tonight. He demanded if I lived there because 'you look suspicious'. I showed my keys and buzzed myself into my building. He left, no apology. This is the reality of Black girls: one day you're called an icon, the next day, a threat." Furthermore, many Black men report that they intuitively smile or hunch their shoulders in the presence of White people, so they are perceived as less physically threatening.

Dr. Joy Degruy explains that centuries of being depicted as criminal, stupid, immoral, and incapable of reasoning in American literature, movies, and news media has programmed all Americans to view African Americans as inferior. Despite existing in a society that perpetuates images of their worthlessness to the mainstream, Black communities continue to promote their own images of excellence and success while making irreplaceable contributions to the American economy and culture. Nevertheless, it remains imperative that the US government acknowledge the physical and psychological pain inflicted on African Americans and take immediate action, on a federal level, to provide compensation for the mental and physical harm caused.

One way the US government can provide appropriate remedy and reparation is to provide free mental and physical health care to all African Americans at every state and federal hospital.

Morally responsible health practitioners can commit to providing African American patients with free or discounted services.

Additionally, governments can work with healthcare providers by granting federal funding to offices that provide free services to African Americans as a form of reparations.

In what other ways do you think governments and morally responsible individuals and institutions in the medical field can provide remedy and reparation to African Americans?

Satisfaction and Guarantees of Non-Repetition

According to the United Nations Basic Principles and Guidelines on the Right to a Remedy and Reparation, satisfaction should include, when appropriate, any or all of the following: taking effective measures towards stopping any continuing violations; verification of the facts and full public disclosure of the truth;

assistance in the search for, recovery, identification and reburial of the victim's bodies in accordance with their own cultural practices; an official declaration or a judicial decision restoring their dignity, reputation and rights; a public apology including acknowledgment of the facts and acceptance of responsibility; penalty for those responsible for the violations; tributes to the victims; and international humanitarian law training in educational material at all levels.

Guarantees of Non-Repetition should include, when appropriate, any or all of the following: strengthening the independence of the victim's justice system; protecting victims in legal, healthcare, media, and human rights professions; providing society education on a continual basis of human rights and international humanitarian law; promoting and enforcing codes of conduct and ethical norms for public servants, law enforcement, correctional officers, economic enterprises, as well as media, medical, psychological, social service and military personnel; promoting mechanisms for preventing social conflicts and mechanisms for their resolutions; and reforming laws contributing to or allowing the human rights violations to happen.

To restore the social dignity of African Americans, take accountability for the harm caused and prove remorse, America must take action towards transformation. Measurable and recorded action must be taken to ensure that slavery, targeted incarceration, institutionalized racism, and a system that grants privileges to one race over another will not continue. The entire criminal justice system needs to be transformed and/or replaced. The bodies discarded in unmarked burial grounds need to be identified and honored. How can we pay tribute to the labor and inventions that former slaves contributed to the United States? What kind of apology can be sufficient for the heinous crimes committed against Black people?

Replace the Current Criminal Justice System
The criminal "justice" system in the United States is an extension of a business model intended to target and incarcerate African Americans for profit and sustain businesses reliant on free labor. The business of incarcerating society's undesirable citizens was so successful that it expanded outside the Black community to include all races. Although the business of mass incarceration continues to disproportionately affect Black Americans, overall, it is a shameful and gross human rights violation affecting all Americans.

It may be possible to get rid of corrupt police chiefs, fire racist police, shame officers for murder, and have police engage more in the community. Still, it is very unlikely that a system rooted in corruption and intended to victimize Black people can be reformed or transformed. If the United States wants to eliminate corruption and racial bias from the justice system, if we want to make communities safer, and honor the pledge of being a nation with liberty and justice for all... the entire system needs to be replaced.

The energy politicians put into being "tough on crime" should be directed into problem-solving. The US has an over 50% recidivism rate - two out of three prisoners return to prison within three years of being released. This is because prisons are heavily focused on punishment instead of reform. The only effective form of satisfaction and guarantee that this will not continue is for the United States to create entirely new systems and processes for dealing with crime, mental illness, and substance abuse - systems rooted in a value system of having respect for humanity. Public servants on every level and in every field should receive cultural education and training to ensure that new systems will not become re-infected with racial bias. They should be required to demonstrate an understanding of the United States' history of upholding White supremacy and their role in creating a more equitable society. Every step of the way, every action and effort should be taken to operate with compassion and intention to provide equally fair treatment to all.

When recreating new justice systems, it is vital to restructure how we respond to and treat drug addiction and mental illness. A report released by the Center on Addiction in 2010 revealed that 65% of prisoners had a substance use disorder (SUD). Of the 35% without a SUD, 20% were under the influence of drugs or alcohol when they committed their crime. In fact, the study found that alcohol and other drugs are significant factors in all crimes, including 78% of violent crimes. Furthermore, according to the Washington Post database on fatal shootings by on-duty police officers, one in five people shot and killed by police officers are mentally ill. If the United States began to treat mental illness episodes and drug addiction as wellness issues, the prison population would immediately be significantly reduced.

When it comes to the justice system, the only path forward is intense education and evaluation of systems and staff at every level. There should be a thorough examination and awareness of how a criminal class is created and perpetuated through school-to-prison pipelines, implicit biases, and a false sense of fear. Everyone needs to be educated on the true history of the United States justice system and how it evolved over time. They should be required to demonstrate a clear understanding of why the US decided to create new systems. They must understand that the new systems they operate in were designed in opposition to the previous system. And every measure possible should be taken to ensure that methods of the past will not be re-implemented.

When it comes to crime and punishment, many other developed countries have proven effective models that can serve as inspiration for new systems in the US. One example is Norway. At one point, Norway prisons were experiencing riots, high rates of recidivism, and even two correction officers were murdered. Instead of cracking down harder and removing prisoner's rights, Norway leaders chose to re-examine their entire system and reform both their morals and approach to dealing with crime. Their new goal is for inmates to learn how to be better neighbors and community members when released. Instead of focusing on punishing people who commit crimes, they began focusing on rehabilitation. They eliminated life sentences. The staff and programming operate with the core basic principles of normality, human dignity, dynamic staff, and reintegration. Life in prison is made to resemble the outside world as much as possible, and courses are taught in socializing and self-defense. They work jobs and are given other duties that encourage responsible decision-making. Essentially, they are learning and practicing how to cooperate peacefully and normally within society. Prison guards are trained to engage with inmates as much as possible and serve more as mentors than punishment-enforcers. Punishment is given by the judge in the courtroom. Being isolated from friends, family, and society is the punishment - but they still have all their rights. Furthermore, prisoners are reintroduced into the workforce well before their release. As a result, there has been a 40% increase in employment rates, and the recidivism rate dropped from around 70% to 20% - the lowest recidivism rate in the world. According to Norwegian researchers, many prisoners turn to crime due to the lack of employment opportunities. Reducing the population of prisoners who are re-incarcerated increases the number of individuals able to contribute to Norway's economy. Prisoners who once felt a sense of hopelessness, report feeling more empowered after receiving the valuable life skills they need to succeed in society and the workforce.

How do you think the US can dismantle prison systems and recreate a successful approach to rehabilitation and reform?

How do you think the US can better respond to drug abuse to prevent drug-related crimes?

What ways do you think we can identify and respond to mental health episodes and provide treatment instead of jail time?

How do you think we can individually and collectively eliminate fear-based stigmas and associations of Black people being dangerous?

Truth Telling, Accountability, and Educational Transformation
The true impact of the slavery industry on America's wealth building and the solid economic foundation it built is glossed over and even omitted in most US history lessons. The history of the United States taught to US citizens was written by White men who depict themselves as underdogs with heroic bravery. They are described as men who explored, innovated, and took the initiative to lead a modern civilization toward a more humane future. However dignified, rational, passionate, or violent, the White men who dominate US history are almost always portrayed as strong and moral, tried but true. They are honored with respect for taking whatever necessary action that made the US as powerful as it is today. Powerful enough to clear a race of indigenous people from their home, enslave Africans, move them across an ocean, emancipate themselves from Great Britain, and build one of the world's most successful countries. The US history taught to citizens in schools is a perfect example of systematic White supremacy and how colonization is still practiced in modern society.

An old Igbo proverb warns, "Until the lions have their own historians, the history of the hunt will always glorify the hunter." To rid ourselves of institutional White supremacy and guarantee that it will not be replaced with another racial hierarchy, we have to take accountability for the facts of our history from the point of view of everyone who was there.

To truly learn how Black people are affected by White supremacy, we need to hear their stories and learn directly from them how it impacts their quality of life. General history books should include a collection of historical accounts from a particular period, and should be taught as such - his story and her story. Not just a White man's recorded stories taught as fact. Transforming the way United States' history is taught - while including the diverse perspectives and stories of all groups - would provide much needed satisfaction to everyone who has had their history erased, distorted, and have subliminally learned that they are part of an inferior race.

Truth-telling hearings have historically been conducted after a human rights violation. They can be immensely healing for communities. These hearings allow oppressed communities an uninterrupted platform to share their truth and provide guidance on which methods of restorative justice will be most impactful. Meanwhile, these hearings are a space for the community that perpetrated or benefited from the violation to sit back and listen - to gain an understanding of how they inflict harm and the effect it has. At some truth-telling hearings, both the perpetrating community and the victimized community will share their accounts of the story. They intentionally confront and acknowledge the suffering caused, then the victims decide what form of repair will be most effective. In other cases, only the victimized community will be present to speak so that their story is not influenced or intimidated by the perpetrators. Likewise, the perpetrators are protected from the possibility of retaliation. The community of those who perpetrated or benefited from the violation would then be encouraged to watch a video of the hearing and have a person from the victimized community lead a discussion on accountability, healing, and ways to remedy the harm.

When South Africa ended their legal apartheid, the country held a nationwide Truth and Reconciliation Commission. White perpetrators of violence were offered amnesty to publicly acknowledge their offenses, and Black people bravely shared their stories explaining how those actions were traumatic for them. It was an opportunity for White people to take accountability and ask for forgiveness - and for the stories of Black people to be heard and validated. The South African Truth and Reconciliation Commission has been reported as highly successful in creating a more accurate account of historical records and opening up the dialogue about race in the country. However, the commission was also considered a massive failure for not giving everyone who wanted to share their story the opportunity to speak. Amnesty and adequate safety from retaliation for those who committed unlawful and violent acts were not upheld. And worst of all, effective measures were not taken to provide economic justice. Even though the apartheid is legally over, racism, institutionalized discrimination, and wealth inequalities persist. There are many ways the US can learn from South Africa's successes and failures.

It is very common for White people in the United States to be willfully unaware that we are operating in systems of White supremacy. Most White Americans have no accountability for participating and perpetuating a racial hierarchy in society. Many completely deny that a racial hierarchy and White privilege even exist. There are, however, a lot of White people who do acknowledge their White privilege, but true allyship is in taking action - choosing fairness over their own ego. The only way Black people can truly believe that the US is committed to ending cycles of racism and discrimination is for the US government, White individuals, and US institutions to take public accountability, commit to ending the cycle, and prove it with their actions. To provide remedy and repair for Black communities and commit to values of racial equality for everyone, there needs to be a sincere apology and transformation of how US history is taught.

The US president and other political leaders must publicly acknowledge that even though past leaders condoned slavery, racism, and segregation, these choices do not reflect the legacy of values we wish to continue. It should be made plainly clear, to everyone, that the US values racial and cultural diversity and will begin redefining society in a way that equally serves, protects, and values all citizens.

History books and curriculum should be revised at every school - and at every grade level - to ensure that students receive a more accurate education about the contributions made by African Americans to the country and the true impact of slavery in establishing the nation's economy.

N'COBRA proposes that an effective and appropriate form of satisfaction is for both the media and history books to include more African American history told from the perspective of African Americans. Additionally, the US government and morally responsible individuals, institutions, and organizations can provide funding for African American filmmakers to create films about Black heroes and heroines, Black people in science, engineering, business, and other historical accounts.

It is also important that all students learn about International Human Rights Law and the United States' commitment to protecting human rights and providing remedy and reparation. Teaching young Americans - future citizens and leaders - the values by which the US governs itself will reduce the risk of repeating mistakes made with disregard for human life.

In memory of Michael Brown Jr., a year after his murder, The Truth Telling Project held a weekend-long truth-telling hearing in Ferguson, Missouri. Families who were directly affected by fatal police shootings were given a stage to share their stories and how they were affected. Workshops were held to provide education about the causes of systematic violence. Local wellness practitioners held space for healing. And Angela Davis, a well-known civil rights activist, shared encouraging words of inspiration. The following week, The Truth Telling Project facilitated "A Night of a Thousand Conversations," a nationwide series of private events where White communities were able to watch and listen to the hearings. Afterward, they participated in guided discussions and honest conversations. These conversations were a safe space for White people to ask whatever questions needed to gain a deeper understanding of how African Americans experience police, how police violence affects Black communities, and how they could take action to create local change. This is an excellent example of how communities can come together and hold space for truth-telling and racial healing.

What are some other ways you think the US government and communities can provide satisfaction through truth-telling?

In what other ways can government, institutions, and businesses take accountability for perpetuating White supremacy as a form of reparations?

Public Memorials and Tributes

The United States would not be what it is today without the willing and unwilling contributions of African Americans. Black people are to thank for the labor and nurture of this country. They have been designing, building, farming, cooking, sewing, entertaining, inventing, and much more since the colonial era.

If you look closely, you will uncover that African Americans are behind many American contributions to the world. Including the invention of tools that revolutionized transportation, like the steamboat propeller invented by Benjamin Montgomery. And even childhood treasures, like the super soaker created by Lonnie Johnson. The Use of black bodies is responsible for many vital medical advances. For example, when doctors discovered that 31-year-old Henrietta Lacks' cancer cells could live and infinitely and multiply very easily outside of the body, they saw an opportunity and extracted her cells for medical research. Previously, medical research was a very slow process because cells would die before significant research could be conducted. But Henrietta Lacks' "HeLa" cells continue to live on and are responsible for a lot of medical breakthroughs - including the research for developing a vaccine for COVID-19 and other diseases. Although Henrietta's cells were extracted without her knowledge, they are the only "immortal cells" to ever be discovered - and they are celebrated internationally as one of the most significant contributions to the medical field.

As far back as the 1600s, Black people have been used to create the infrastructure of the US by clearing forests, building homes, and entire cities - including colonial New Amsterdam, now known as New York City. Even the Wall Street wall was built by slaves in 1664 and was the site of the largest slave trade market in the country until 1762. Later, the New York Stock Exchange was created and operated on the same street. At the time, Africans were considered heathens, so when someone died - or several hundred were killed to prevent a revolt - they would be buried just outside the city's limits. As New York City continued to grow and expand, this African cemetery was paved over and forgotten. The graveyard remained out of sight and out of mind, until 1991 when developers began constructing a federal office building over it. While excavating the land, construction workers found several thousand human remains. They discovered that the bones of the slaves that built Wall Street are still buried beneath it. As word spread about the skeleton remains, activists and community members began advocating for their preservation. Then, in 1993 US Congress declared the site a National Historic Landmark. In 2003, a monument was created on the site, and in 2006 President George Bush declared the site a National Monument. Visit New York City today, located at 290 Broadway on the corner of Elk and Duane. There, you will find the African Burial Ground National Monument - a large monument aside grassy mounds that mark where tens of thousands of once-forgotten African Americans rest. This monument is an excellent example of how the US government can sponsor memorials as a form of reparations. Paying respect to the slaves who contributed to the very land they were buried on is very satisfying.

A few organizations have begun to identify the many slave burial grounds that exist throughout the US. Still, without sufficient funding, it is challenging to organize and execute such efforts. One way governments and individuals can pay respect for the African Americans who contributed to their community is to fund the Black organizations that are locating unmarked burial sites and commission Black artists to create a monument where they lay.

Public memorials and monuments that pay tribute to enslaved Africans are an invaluable way of showing respect for their contributions. More than just a form of satisfaction, the inclusion of African American memorials and statues serve as a reminder to all Americans that everyone's contribution is valued. However dark the circumstances, the US has always been a pool of diversity. It is evident in the array of infrastructure and design. The White men memorialized in the downtown area of every major city are not the only people the US have to celebrate. There are men and women of many backgrounds who have equally impacted this country. The contributions of slaves and other African Americans have been deliberately erased to promote a narrative of White superiority. One way to remedy that harm is to intentionally create and fund monuments honoring the life and sacrifices made by our African American forefathers.

For example, in Boston's South End - at the corner of West Newton Street and Columbus Avenue - you will find Harriet Tubman Square, the location of the Emancipation sculpture created by Meta Vaux Warrick. The statue was created in 1913 to celebrate the 50th anniversary of the Emancipation Proclamation. In the same location, the city recently added the Harriet Tubman Trail, which uses public art to represent how the African American experience exemplifies America's quest for freedom, equality, and justice.

Another effective way to pay tribute as a form of remedy and repair is for governments to fund research efforts to identify the inventions of slaves that were not allowed to be patented, or that were attributed to a White person. The patent should then be transferred into the name of its rightful creator and its royalties given to the inventor's descendants.
Educators and students can dive a little deeper into the history of their school to examine if there are any notable African Americans who contributed to their school. Or if there is any uncovered African American history that should be memorialized and remembered.

Morally responsible individuals and communities can do their own research to identify how African Americans contributed to their local area. They can work together to identify Black artists and designers and then commission them to create memorials as tribute.

What other ways can governments, individuals, institutions, and businesses publicly pay tribute to the contributions made to their community by African Americans?

Thank you.

Sources & Recommended Reading

One
INTRODUCING... REPARATIONS.

"Constitution of the United States," Preamble | WhiteHouse.gov

National Coalition of Blacks for Reparations in America | NCOBRAonline.org

Anthony Phillips | "Haiti, France and the Independence Debt of 1895" | The Canada-Haiti Information Project | 2008 | canada-haiti.ca

"The District of Columbia Emancipation Act" | National Archives | archives.gov

"Compensation and Reparations for the Evacuation, Relocation, and Internment Index" | National Archives | archives.gov

Universal Declaration of Human Rights | UN.org

"Search the Compensation and Reparations for the Evacuation, Relocation, and Internment Index (Redress Case Files)" | National Archives | archives.gov

Basic Principles and Guidelines on the Right to a Remedy and Reparation for Victims of Gross Violations of International Human Rights Law and Serious Violations of International Humanitarian Law | ohchr.org

Allen J. Davis | "Historical Timeline of Reparations Payments Made From 1783 through 2021 by the United States Government, States, Cities, Religious Institutions, Colleges and Universities, and Corporations" | UMassAmherst | guides.library.umass.edu/reparations

H.R.40 - Commission to Study and Develop Reparation Proposals for African-Americans Act | congress.gov

Two
AMERICA'S FOUNDATION OF WEALTH

Edward E. Baptist | *The Half Has Never Been Told: Slavery and the Making of American Capitalism* | Basic Books | 2016

Gene Dattel | *Cotton and Race In the Making Of America: The Human Costs of Economic Power* | Government Institutes | 2009

Eric Williams | *Capitalism and Slavery* | University of North Carolina Press | 1944

P. Scott Corbett, Volker Janssen, John M. Lund, Todd Pfannestiel, Sylvie Waskiewicz, Paul Vickery | "The Economics of Cotton" | OpenStax American History Textbook | 2014 | lumenlearning.com

Henry Louis Gates, Jr. | "Why Was Cotton 'King'" | 100 Amazing Facts About the Negro No.17 | 2013 | theroot.com

Sven Beckert, Seth Rockman | *Slavery's Capitalism: A New History of American Economic Development* | University of Pennsylvania Press | 2016

Joshua D. Rothman | *Flush Times and Fever Dreams: A Story of Capitalism and Slavery in the Age of Jackson* | University of Georgia Press | 2012

Jonathan Daniel Wells | *The Kidnapping Club: Wall Street, Slavery, and Resistance on the Eve of the Civil War* | Bold Type Books | 2020

Martha A. Sandweiss, Craig Hollander | "Princeton and Slavery: Holding the Center" | The Princeton and Slavery Project | slavery.princeton.edu

Katie Reilly | "This is How Columbia University Benefited from Slavery" | TIME Magazine | 2017 | time.com

Helene Van Rossum | "How Rutgers University is Connected to Sojourner Truth: The Hardenbergh family in Ulster County, NY" | What Exit? New Jerseyana at Rutgers University Special Collections and University Archives | 2017 | sinclairnj.blogs.rutgers.edu

"King's College and Slavery" | Columbia University | columbiaandslavery.columbia.edu

"Scarlet and Black" | Rutgers University | scarlettandblack.rutgers.edu

Sources & Recommended Reading

Three
THE JIM CROW ERA

"African American Records: Freedmen's Bureau," African American Heritage | National Archives | archives.gov

"Freedman's Bank Building" | US Department of the Treasury | treasury.gov

The 14th Amendment | constitution.congress.gov

The Fifteenth Amendment | constitution.congress.gov

R. Christopher Whalen | *Inflated: How Money and Debt Built the American Dream* | John Wiley & Sons | 2010

Elmus Wicker | *Banking panics of the Gilded Age* | Cambridge University Press | 2000

Richard White | "The Rise of Industrial America, 1877-1900" | The Gilder Lehrman Institute of American History | gilderlehrman.org

Frederick Douglass | *The Life and Times of Frederick Douglass* | Park Publishing Company | 1881

"Black Code," United States History | Britannica | britannica.com

"Slave Codes" | U.S. History Online Textbook | ushistory.org

Douglas A. Blackmon | *Slavery by Another Name: The Re-Enslavement of Black Americans from the Civil War to World War II* | Anchor Books | 2008

Nancy O'Brien Wagner, Bluestem Heritage Group | "Slavery by Another Name History Background" | Slavery By Another Name | bento.cdn.pbs.org

"U.S. Reports: United States v. Cruikshank et al., 92 U.S. 542 (1876)" | Library of Congress | loc.gov

"Landmark Legislation: Civil Rights Act of 1875" | United States Senate | senate.gov

"Plessy v. Ferguson: Primary Documents in American History" | Library of Congress | loc.gov

"Jim Crow Museum of Racist Memorabilia" | Ferris State University | ferris.edu

"President Franklin Delano Roosevelt and the New Deal" | Library of Congress | loc.gov

Michael Honey | "A Dream Deferred: After bloody battles for desegregation, blacks in Memphis are still behind" | The Nation | 2004 | thenation.com

Larry Tye | *Rising from the Rails, Pullman Porters and the Making of the Black Middle Class* | Henry Holt and Company | 2005

Patricia Hill Collins | "Gender, Black Feminism, and Black Political Economy" | Annals of the American Academy of Political and Social Science | 2000

Ruth Thompson Miller | "Legal Segregation: Racial Violence and the Long Term Implications" | Texas A&M University | 2006

George M. Frederickson | *The Black Image in the White Mind: The Debate on Afro-American Character and Destiny* | Harper and Row | 1971

Carter G. Woodson | *The Miseducation of the Negro* | Carter G. Woodson | 1933

Mark E. Dudley | *Brown v. Board of Education (1954)* | Lerner Publishing Group | 1997

"The Plessy Decision," History- Brown v Board of Education Re-enactment | United States Courts | uscourts.gov

Ruth Thompson-Miller | *Jim Crow's Legacy: The Lasting Impact of Segregation* | Rowman and Littlefield | 2014

Rachel Yehuda, Amy Lehrner | "Intergenerational Transmission of Trauma Effects: Putative Role of Epigenetic Mechanisms" | World Psychiatry Volume 17, Issue 3 | 2018 | onlinelibrary.wiley.com

Four
EXODUS: THE GREAT MIGRATION

Isabel Wilkerson | "The Long-Lasting Legacy of the Great Migration" | Smithsonian Magazine | 2016 | smithsonianmag.com

Isabel Wilkerson | *The Warmth of Other Suns: The Epic Story of America's Great Migration* | Penguin Books Limited | 2010

James W. Lowen | *Sundown Towns: A Hidden Dimension of American Racism* | The New Press | 2005

"Mapping Prejudice" | University of Michigan | mappingprejudice.umn.edu

Sources & Recommended Reading

Four
GENOCIDE

Dwight Callahan | *The Talking Book: African Americans and the Bible* | Yale University Press | 2008

"Convention on the Prevention and Punishment of the Crime of Genocide," Article II | the United Nation | 1948 | un.org

"Lynching in America" | The Equal Justice Initiative | lynchinginamerica.eji.org

Ida. B. Wells | *Crusade for Justice: The Autobiography of Ida B. Wells* | University of Chicago Press | 1970

Allen W. Trelease | *White Terror: The Ku Klux Klan Conspiracy and Southern Reconstruction* | Greenwood Press | 1971

Charles Seguin, David Rigby | "National Crimes: A New National Data Set of Lynchings in the United States, 1883 to 1941" | Sociological Research for a Dynamic World | 2019 | journals.sagepub.com

"Lynchings: By State and Race, 1882-1968," Lynchings Stats Year Dates Causes | Tuskegee University | archive.tuskegee.edu

"The Murder of Emmitt Till" | Library of Congress | loc.gov

Dave Tell | "The 'Shocking Story' of Emmett Till and the Politics of Public Confession" | Quarterly Journal of Speech | 2008

H.R.35 Emmett Till Antilynching Act | congress.gov

Billie Holiday | "Strange Fruit" | Youtube

Robin Lally | "Police Use of Fatal Force Identified as a Leading Cause of Death in Young Men" | Rutgers University | 2019 | rutgers.edu

"What Happened in Ferguson?" | The New York Times | nytimes.com

Mapping Police Violence | mappingpoliceviolence.org

Leslie M. Harris | *In the Shadow of Slavery: African Americans in New York City, 1626-1863* | University Chicago Press | 2004

"An Absolute Massacre" – The New Orleans Slaughter of July 30, 1866" | National Park Services | nps.gov

Calvin Schermerhorn | "Civil-Rights Laws Don't Always Stop Racism: Although

Sources & Recommended Reading

the 1866 Memphis Massacre Happened 150 Years Ago, it Still Has a Powerful Legacy in the South." | The Atlantic | 2016 | theatlantic.com

Kevin R. Hardwick | *Your Old Father Abe Lincoln Is Dead and Damned* | Oxford University Press | 1993

"Atlanta Riot of 1906" | Britannica | britannica.org

Olivia B. Waxman | "'It Just Goes On and On': How the Race Riots of 1919's 'Red Summer' Helped Shape a Century of American History" | TIME Magazine| 2019 | time.com

Scott Ellsworth | *Death in a Promised Land: The Tulsa Race Riot of 1921* | Louisiana State University Press | 1982

"Detroit Race Riot (1943)" | Black Past | BlackPast.org

"Detroit Race Riot (1967)" | Black Past | BlackPast.org

"U.S. Public Health Service Syphilis Study at TuskegeeU.S. Public Health Service Syphilis Study at Tuskegee" | Center for Disease Control and Prevention | cdc.gov

Lutz Kaelber | Eugenics: Compulsory Sterilization in 50 American States | uvm.edu

Johanna Schoen | *Choice and Coercion: Birth Control, Sterilization, and Abortion in Public Health Welfare* | University of North Carolina Press | 2005

Lisa Armstrong | "Sterilized by the State" | Volume 32, Number 7 | Essence Magazine | April 2012

Gregory N. Price, William Darity Jr., Rhonda V. Sharpe | "Did North Carolina Economically Breed-Out Blacks During its Historical Eugenic Sterilization Campaign?" | American Review of Political Economy | 2020

"Infant Mortality," Reproductive Health | Centers for Disease Control and Prevention | cdc.gov

Five
SLAVERY EVOLVED: THE US CRIMINAL JUSTICE SYSTEM

"Following the Money of Mass Incarceration" | Prison Policy Initiative | prisonpolicy.org

The 13th Amendment | constitution.congress.gov

Sources & Recommended Reading

Margaret Werner Cahalan, Lee Anne Parsons | "Historical Corrections Statistics in the United States, 1850-1984" | U.S. Department of Justice Bureau of Justice Statistics | 1986

Norm Stamper | *Breaking Rank: A Top Cop's Exposé of the Dark Side of American Policing* | Nation Books | 2005

"Stop and Frisk Data" | ACLU of New York | nyclu.org

Elliott Hannon | "Leaked Audio Captures Bloomberg Defending Racial Profiling and Stop-and-Frisk Policing" | Slate Magazine | 2020 | slate.com

Mancini, Matthew J. | *One Dies, Get Another: Convict Leasing in the American South, 1866-1928* | University of South Carolina Press | 1996

Whitney Benns | "American Slavery, Reinvented" | The Atlantic | 2015 | theatlantic.com

Antoinette Harrell | *Department of Justice: Slavery, Peonage, and Involuntary Servitude* | Antoinette Harrell | 2014

Dan Baum | "Legalize It All: How to Win the War on Drugs" | Harper's Magazine | harpers.org

H.R.5269 - Comprehensive Crime Control Act of 1990 | congress.gov

H.R.5210 - Anti-Drug Abuse Act of 1988 | congress.gov

H.R.3355 - Violent Crime Control and Law Enforcement Act of 1994 | congress.gov

"Help Us End Bail Bonds!" | Color of Change | colorofchange.org

Benjamin Weiser | "Kalief Browder's Suicide Brought Changes to Rikers. Now It Has Led to a $3 Million Settlement" | The New York Times | 2019 | nytimes.com

"Kalief Browder, in His Own Words" | The New Yorker | 2016 | thenewyorker.com

Christopher Mathias | "Here's Kalief Browder's Heartbreaking Research Paper On Solitary Confinement" | Huff Post | 2015 | huffpost.com

Sources & Recommended Reading

Six
STUNTED GROWTH: EXPLORING THE RACIAL WEALTH GAP

Neil Bhutta, Andrew C. Chang, Lisa J. Dettling, and Joanne W. Hsu with assistance from Julia Hewitt | "Disparities in Wealth by Race and Ethnicity in the 2019 Survey of Consumer Finances" | Board of Governors of the Federal Reserve System | 2020 | federalreserve.gov

Moritz Kuhn, Moritz Schularick, Ulrike I. Steins | "Income and Wealth Inequality in America, 1949-2016" | Federal Reserve Bank of Minneapolis | 2018 | minneapolisfed.org

Thomas Shapiro, Tatjana Meschede, Sam Osoro | "The Roots of the Widening Racial Wealth Gap: Explaining the Black-White Economic Divide" | Institute on Assets and Social Policy | 2013 | heller.brandeis.edu

Dedrick Asante-Muhammed, Chuck Collins, Josh Hoxie and Emanuel Nieves | "Ever-Growing Gap: Without Change, African-American and Latino Families Won't Match White Wealth for Centuries" | Institute for Policy Studies | 2016 | ips-dc.org

William Darity Jr., Darrick Hamilton, Mark Paul, Alan Aja, Anne Price, Antonio Moore, Caterina Chiopris | "What We Get Wrong About Closing the Racial Wealth Gap" | Samuel DuBois Cook Center on Social Equity and Insight Center for Community Economic Development | 2018 | socialequity.duke.edu

Black Owned Businesses Statistics | blackdemographics.com

Claire Kramer Mills, Jessica Battisto | "Double Jeopardy: COVID 19's Concentrated Health and Wealth Effects in Black Communities" | Federal Reserve Bank of New York | 2020 | newyorkfed.org

Black-owned businesses received less than 2% of PPP loans while white-owned businesses received 83% | thebusinessofbusiness.com

"Data Point: 2019 Mortgage Market Activity and Trends" | Consumer Financial Protection Bureau | 2020 | files.consumerfinance.gov

Sibylle Scholz, Chrissi Jackson | "Restitution for American Slavery: A Forensic Economics Approach" | 2019 | reparationshandbook.com

Ta-Nehisi Coates | "A Case for Reparations" | The Atlantic | 2014 | theatlantic.com

Richard Kluckow | "The Impact of Heir Property on Post-Katrina Housing Recovery in New Orleans" | Colorado State University | 2014

Sources & Recommended Reading

Annie Nova | "The Student Debt Crisis Has Hit Black Students Especially Hard. Here's How." | CNBC: Personal Finance | 2019 | cnbc.com

Jacob W. Faber | "Racial Dynamics of Subprime Mortgage Lending at the Peak" | Housing Policy Debate | 2013 | jacobfaber.com

Three-Fifths Compromise | Britannica | britannica.com

Nancy Joan Weiss | *Farewell to the Party of Lincoln: Black Politics in the Age of F.D.R* | Princeton University Press | 1983

Alex Tausanovitch and Danielle Root | "How Partisan Gerrymandering Limits Voting Rights" | Center for American Progress | 2020 | americanprogress.org

Eight
A PATH FORWARD

William Tecumseh Sherman | *Memoirs of General William Tecumseh Sherman* | Penguin Random House | 2000

"Landmark Legislation: The Homestead Act of 1862," The Civil War: The Senate's Story | the United States Senate | senate.gov

Rosanna Xia | "Manhattan Beach Was Once Home to Black Beachgoers, but The City Ran Them Out. Now it Faces a Reckoning" | Los Angeles Times | latimes.com

The Bill of Rights | archives.gov

"Legislative Corner" | Voice Of The Experienced | vote-nola.org

"Researching African American Ancestors" | Search and Records | ancestry.com

23andMe's State-of-the-Art Geographic Ancestry Analysis | 23andme.com

"To Fulfill These Rights" | Lyndon B. Johnson | Commencement Address at Howard University | 1965

"Executive Order 11246" | US Department of Labor | dol.gov

"The Bill of Rights" | America's Founding Documents | archives.gov

Sources & Recommended Reading

"Being Black in Corporate America: An Intersectional Exploration" | COQUAL | 2019 | cocqual.org

Fidan Ana Kurtulus | "The Impact of Affirmative Action on the Employment of Minorities and Women over Three Decades: 1973-2003" | W.E. Upjohn Institute for Employment Research | 2015 | research.upjohn.org
Ana Patricia Muñoz, Marlene Kim, Mariko Chang, Regine O. Jackson, Darrick Hamilton, William A. Darity Jr. | "The Color of Wealth in Boston" | Federal Reserve Bank of Boston | 2015 | bostonfed.org

Sibylle Scholz, Chrissi Jackson | "Restitution for American Slavery: A Forensic Economics Approach" | 2019 | reparationshandbook.com

William A. Darity and A. Kirsten Mullen | *From Here to Equality: Reparations for Black Americans in the Twenty-First Century* | the University of North Carolina Press | 2020

Dorian T. Warren | "Minimum Livable Wage Policy Brief" | The Movement for Black Lives | m4bl.org

"Booker, Pressley Reintroduce "Baby Bonds" Legislation to Combat Wealth Inequality" | Corey Booker | 2019 | booker.senate.gov

Voting Rights | Voice Of The Experienced | vote-nola.org/voting-rights

"Status and Trends in the Education of Racial and Ethnic Minorities" | National Center for Educational Statistics | 2010 | nces.ed.gov

"Trends in College Pricing & Student Aid 2020" | College Board | 2020 | research.collegeboard.org

"Georgetown Reflects on Slavery, Memory, and Reconciliation" | Georgetown University | georgetown.edu/slavery

Matthew Quallen | "Slavery Inextricably Tied To Georgetown's Growth" | The Hoya | 2015 | thehoya.com

"The Value of Historically Black Colleges and Universities" | United Negro College Fund, National Admission for College Admission and Counseling | nacacnet.org

"Historically Black Colleges & Universities" | Thurgood Marshall College Fund | tmcf.org

Sources & Recommended Reading

Kesi Foster, Montague Simmons | "Free College Education Policy Brief" | The Movement for Black Lives | m4bl.org

Joy Degruy | *Post Traumatic Slave Syndrome* | Uptone Press | 2005

"Fatal Force" | The Washington Post | thewashingtonpost.com

Michael Tonry, Editor | *Crime and Justice, Volume 42: Crime and Justice in America: 1975-2025* | University of Chicago Press | 2013

"Behind Bars II: Substance Abuse and America's Prison Population" | National Center on Addiction and Substance Abuse at Columbia University | 2010 | ojp.gov

"Criminal Justice Drug Facts" | National Institute on Drug Abuse | drugabuse.gov

David Marchese | "What Can America Learn From South Africa About National Healing?" | The New York Times | 2020 | nytimes.com

Alex Boraine | *A Country Unmasked: Inside South Africa's Truth and Reconciliation Commission* | Oxford University Press | 2001

Desmond Tutu | *No Future Without Forgiveness* | The Crown Publishing Group | 1999

"What is Reparations?" | NCOBRA | ncobraonline.com/reparations

"Violence in America: Exposure Through Truth-Telling," Previous Events | The Truth Telling Project | thetruthtellingproject.org/events

"America's always Had Black Inventors – Even When the Patent System Explicitly Excluded Them" | The Conversation | theconversation.com

Noel Jackson | "Vessels for Collective Progress: the Use of HeLa cells in COVID-19 research" | Harvard Graduate School of the Arts and Sciences | 2020 | sitn.hms.harvard.edu

Zoe Thomas | "The Hidden Links Between Slavery and Wall Street" | BBC News | 2019 | bbc.com

Sources & Recommended Reading

"A Sacred Space in Manhattan," African Burial Ground | National Park Service | nps.gov

"Emancipation: A Statue and A Trail" | Boston Women's Heritage Trail | bwht.org

Sources & Recommended Reading

Made in the USA
Columbia, SC
24 March 2022